ARMCHAIR MILLIONAIRE

ARMCHAIR MILLIONAIRE

by
Fred Hal Vice

Paladin Press
Boulder, Colorado

Armchair Millionaire

Published by Paladin Press, a division of
Paladin Enterprises, Inc., P.O. Box 1307, Boulder, CO 80306

ISBN 0-87364-204-X
Printed in the United States of America

First Edition

Cover art by Robert Warren Taylor

DEDICATION

To all the tens of thousands of people seeking a better way of life, secure and with confidence in the thought that America is still the greatest land of opportunity anywhere in the world.

To my incredibly wise and beautiful wife and my patient daughters, whom I have somewhat neglected while doing research and completing the writing of this book.

Last, but certainly not least, my parents and all the others of my family, teachers, current and past friends and acquaintances, and the so many other people who inspired and encouraged me to fulfill my own destiny, even in the face of troubles and setbacks—to all of those I give my eternal thanks, God bless you.

CONTENTS

PREFACE

Being a great author and writing a masterpiece of great literary art is a highly improbable goal for me. My basic intent is to give you the facts as I know them from observation, investigation, interview, and even from my own personal experiences. I have attempted to do this using expressions and explanations that everyone should easily and immediately understand or relate to. If, through my efforts, some people become happier, more secure and confident through gaining a knowledge they theretofore had not possessed, then I will feel a great sense of pride and accomplishment.

For too many years I also was trapped in a world demanding so much of my time that I could consider little else than working and living day by day. *Too many of us are so busy making pennies that we have no time to make real dollars.* All too soon we wind up sixty-five years old with a nagging sense of wasted years and lost opportunities. We live out the remainder of our time wondering what happened to our dreams and our youth.

It is perfectly obvious that extremely wealthy people are not ten times smarter than anyone else—that is a mental impossibility; they do not work ten times harder—that is a physical impossibility. Then why the great difference in level of wealth? Simply because they are possessors of the key. I call that key, **MMM: M**ental **M**aneuverability and **M**anipulation. They may have made a supreme effort to learn, or stumbled over it, or had it passed down to them. In any regard they have it, and *it does work.*

Webster's Dictionary defines the key terms of **MMM** as follows:

> **Mental:** Of or related to the mind or the total emotional and intellectual response of the individual to his environment.
>
> **Maneuverability:** To bring about or secure as a result of skillful management, to guide with adroitness and design.
>
> **Manipulation:** To change by artful means to serve one's purpose.

These are not full definitions of each of the words, but they are the portions I emphasize to clarify the concept of **MMM**. The key—**M**ental **M**aneuverability and **M**anipulation—as a personal directive to better living can be expressed in the following way:

With all available mental capabilities and judgment, seek information and solid advice, making a determination of what fits your personality, desire, and ability. Always be able and prepared to change the course of action, staying flexible and versatile, but not allowing your ego or others' negativism to interfere with success or progress. After creating a doctrine of personal motivation, become alert to all opportunities around you and be willing to take full advantage of each opportunity in the effort to attain *Armchair Millionaire* status. The bottom line is maintaining honest ethics. When you reach your ultimate goal, you will not only experience tremendous self-satisfaction, but will be able to look anyone in the eye and say, "I am proud of where I am, and how I got here."

MMM is the key I share with you. Take it and use it wisely, help others, listen to others, learn and be tenacious in your efforts. You, too, can possess the key and acquire all that you dream of as *Armchair Millionaires.*

1. THE "MMM" STORY

Nineteen seventy-four and early 1975 were very insecure, threatening, and worrisome years. I had made a decision in 1973 that I had to change my life, or else end up like millions of others; barely existing on social security plus, *maybe*, a small company pension in the so-called Golden Years, which more commonly become the Black Years of survival.

Having a small amount of savings, but no real plan, I left my regular salaried job that at least did get me by month to month. With the mortgage and car payments to keep up, I could enjoy a night on the town as long as I didn't splurge too often. But with rising prices and inflation my income was running a poor second to my obligations. I had noticed in newspapers, magazines, and other advertisements about high-paying careers in sales. So, being very motivated toward avoiding the poorhouse, I resigned my salaried position.

I abandoned that monthly paid albatross-around-my-neck and hit the glittering world of direct sales, which promised huge incomes for just average working abilities and hours. I played it smart, passing by vacuum cleaner sales, pots and pans, encyclopedias and many others. Let me tell you, I went for the really big time, the granddaddy of them all: life insurance sales. I passed all the tests with flying colors; some of the best test grades they had ever seen, so they said. Well, after several weeks of intensive training, which included life insurance history, current methods, sales psychology, motivational lectures, and motivational tapes at night while I slept (with a pillow speaker), I was turned loose on the world. But first, they told me to go see all my relatives, friends, and neighbors. Boy, was I hyped! I knew I had arrived! It wouldn't be long until I reached the pot of gold at the end of the rainbow.

Six months later, after many fourteen-hour days and a number of six- and seven-day weeks, making less than half of the money that I had been making on that old albatross-around-the-neck job, I began to have some doubts about my ability as a life insurance salesman. But, then, I reasoned it probably wasn't my fault; I just wasn't cut out to sell insurance. I would probably do great selling something else. All I had to do was find the right thing.

Eleven months later, after having found several of the right things which ultimately degenerated also, I finally concluded that direct sales, though good for some, was not exactly my cup of tea (at least in the present time and circumstances). I had no choice but to admit total defeat, and my big pot of gold became a tarnished illusion. Well, what would any normal red-blooded human being do in this situation? You guessed it. I swallowed my pride, hung my head, and asked for my old job back. The only problem was they had found a younger person for less money than what they had been paying me.

Shortly thereafter, about one week away from hitting the soup and unemployment line, the fellow upstairs granted me a reprieve. A competitor of the company I had worked for in the salaried job called and said they might have a job for me, and wondered if I would like to come in and interview for it.

Without going into details of the interview, I will sum up the outcome. I was to be the manager of a newly-opened branch office which was not doing well. Because of the limited profit the office was producing and my age (thirty-nine), advanced according to their corporate structure, they would have to start me at a figure of a little over 60% of what I had been making in my previous salaried position, at which I had sixteen years' experience. It all sounded very logical and reasonable (for them, of course). Being somewhat over the barrel, so to speak, and having a firm desire to continue the practice of eating and paying my bills, I accepted their offer.

This could have been the end of the story. In eighteen months I had traveled a complete circle. I had my fling and now was back to working at what I had been doing, complete with a 40% reduction in income. But about ninety days later I made an amazing discovery. Not only was I keeping current on monthly obligations, I was actually accumulating and saving money, too—all on a salary reduced by 40% of what it had been some twenty-one months prior. *I was actually living better and enjoying life more, and I knew why.* In the eighteen months of direct selling I had honed my money management abilities to a fine edge. It was either that or become one of the fatalities in the war between Mr. Average John Q. Public and inflation. In my case, the battle had an added dimension—greatly reduced earnings. I not only had survived, but with the new job (even though reduced in income by 40%) I was showing a significant gain in financial strength. It then occurred to me that I should list in a chronological order all that I had done in the two years past to survive, and then refine those things into a definite plan and method, thus forming the origins of **M**ental **M**aneuverability and **M**anipulation—**MMM.**

I have heard the old cliche over and over again, if you want to be successful "put your nose to the grindstone," among other equally stupid, meaningless, and erroneous tidbits of supposed profoundness, such as, "early to bed, early to rise, makes a man healthy, wealthy and wise." How about those of us who like to go to bed late and get up late? If you want a good chuckle, read the help wanted column. I see many catch phrases such as *hard work, dedication, PMA (Positive Mental Attitude)*, and so on. I saw an employment advertisement that had it all. It went something like this: "*If you're sincere, hardworking, loyal and a positive thinker, we have a career waiting for you.*" Now let's reconstruct what this employer was actually saying. "If you're sincere (*will beg me*); hardworking (*ten, twelve hours a day with no overtime*); loyal (*never look around for a better opportunity, recognize me as God*); a positive thinker (*positive that I am really your creator*); we have a career waiting for you (*I'll pay you a dollar for every four or five you earn for me, then get rid of you when you're of no further use*)."

A friend of mine fell for this line some fifteen years ago, kept his nose clean, put in the long hours, got a nice-sounding title, not a bad annual income if he had been working forty hours a week, but he was working sixty and seventy; an unskilled laborer with overtime would have made more. About two years ago my friend collapsed at his desk with a heart attack produced through job stress. He was recovering when his employer told him it would be in everyone's best interests if he was retired to a less demanding job (at about a third of the pay). Well, he never had to worry about it after that, he had a second heart attack (job-related stress); he died.

A **P**ositive **M**ental **A**ttitude—**PMA** can be one of the greatest assets in the world, but all too often it becomes one of the biggest liabilities. I think everyone has a **PMA** in various degrees and direction. A large number of people have the **PMA** that they are poorer financially or emotionally today than yesterday, and they have excellent reason; it's true, they are. Unfortunately, most of the time it occurs through conditions that they feel they have little or no control over. As an example, your boss was good to you. A year ago he gave you an 8% raise in pay. Now, a year later, inflation is 13%, housing, groceries, etc.; gasoline alone has shot up 26% to 30%. A year ago, you put $2,000.00 in the bank at 6.5% interest. By the time you paid the government taxes on your interest earnings to the tune of about 25%, deduct the 13% inflation figure, your $2,000.00 is worth about $1,824.85. You lost all of your interest, plus $175.15 of your principle, and didn't have to do anything. Let's take a look at your income. You make $18,000.00 a year, got an 8% increase, lost 13% in inflation (13% average; 26–30% on gasoline, higher percentages on meat, coffee, etc., at times; let's use 13%—give them the benefit of the doubt). You wound up with the gross purchasing power of $16,912.28 before taxes. Oh, yes, don't forget to figure 25% off your 8% increase for taxes, which is $360.00 and will leave you with a grand purchasing power of $16,552.28. Well, between your savings and income you lost a total of $1,622.87 for the year. If this continues, in a few years you're going to be a basket case. If that happens, you would be better off quitting your job and going on welfare. All of this should be referred to as the Erosion of Income, Savings, and Individuality Syndrome.

This syndrome not only plays havoc financially, but emotionally. The wife and kids spend too much, good old

Dad doesn't earn enough, the budget gets juggled, Peter is robbed to pay Paul, a second income is required, the wife and mother goes to work, the children lose their respect and guidance, the family faces turmoil, someone gets fed up and bows out to a better life. Financial need is always recognized as one of the leading reasons for family and marital problems, often resulting in the tragedy of broken homes, felonious acts, and long-lasting psychological problems.

A **PMA** is a wonderful thing if it is in the proper perspective with solid direction and confirmed method. The method must allow the time and money to enjoy leisure activities in ways and places of your choice. With all our modern conveniences and technology, not much has been accomplished in shortening the workweek to allow more time for play. Many people still work the long and inconvenient hours that our counterparts did thirty and forty years ago. Ideally we should be working only four to five hours a day with a maximum of four-day workweeks to keep pace with the economy and maintain a decent worry-free lifestyle. For those of us who want more money, it is only right that we should pay a higher price of time or effort through increased hours of application or creative ability, and that is precisely what this book is all about: *how to have more than you have now with less effort* or *how to become rich through better application of your time and ability.* You will find all this possible through creative purchasing and income multiplication, all important parts of **M**ental **M**aneuverability and **M**anipulation, **MMM**.

The following chapters contain many things with which I personally have experienced and have used to my total benefit. Other items are situations, ideas, and theories of common sense origin. If a moneymaking project appeals to you, line up your perspectives and goals and then use it. A good rule of thumb is to bounce the idea off the head of your accountant or attorney, not for their approval, but to find out what your financial exposure or legal liability might be. Finally, don't be afraid to *think big*, as almost all of us have a way of rising to meet the occasion. As you read, take time for reflection. Write down your thoughts and reactions, if it helps consolidate your ideas. Don't worry if your ideas seem to be nothing more than seemingly impossible dreams. Every famous person has dreamed his or her way to important realities.

2. "MMM" *EXAMPLES*

I will now illustrate, by way of example, how **MMM** works.

After three months of direct sales, I had the old-time doldrums. Money was very tight, my buying power zilch. It took everything just to keep a roof over my head. My spirits were at a very low ebb. Then one Sunday, a friend called and insisted that I accompany him to a furniture store to look at a home bar he was interested in purchasing.

HOME BARS FOR HALF-PRICE

At the store I could work up very little interest in his purchase. He paid $450.00 for a luxury item, when I was having a tough time keeping the wolf away from the door. It appeared that there was less than $50.00 in materials used. Most of the cost was in labor, design, wholesaler's and retailer's profit, plus transportation costs to the store; another $8.00 was charged for delivery to his home. A few days later my money-spending friend had several people in, among them myself, and we enjoyed cocktails at his new luxury bar. I could not help noticing the envy and remarks produced by that overpriced piece of furniture. A thought slowly began to materialize.

The following week I made a detailed plan of my friend's bar, checked at lumberyards and material shops for prices, and even wound up with free instruction regarding woodworking, gluing, Formica application, and material cutting and sewing. Just seven days later I called another friend of mine who also had very little extra cash. I asked if he had seen our mutual friend's new bar yet. He replied yes, and I asked him if he would be interested in having one just like it free, plus making some extra money in part-time hours. He practically climbed through the phone with curiosity. I, in turn, invited him and his wife over that evening to discuss it. He, besides being short on money, possessed some power tools we would need and his wife was a pretty fair seamstress. I still had a little money left in my savings account that I could part with for a short time if I was sure of getting it back plus some profit, and I *was* sure. We formulated our plan that evening and the following week put it in effect. On Saturday morning we purchased all the materials we would need from the lumberyard and fabric store. I had been right, the bill was only about $250.00. Whoops! I forgot to tell you, we were building five bars, not just one, therefore spending about $50.00 per bar in materials.

In earlier years I had some exposure to the magic of mass production to lower costs and reduce hours, and as it turned out, we made the five bars in only about twice the time required to make one. When cutting and assembling anything, a lot of time is wasted in setting up machinery, pattern drawing, etc. In our case, instead of just cutting one thing at a time, we were cutting five. The same method applies to assembly finish work, such as cutting and bonding Formica and leather trim. This may sound like it took a lot of time, but it really didn't. Including time to shop for and purchase materials, cutting, assembling and trim, we completed the five bars in a little over seventeen part-time hours. Again, I refer to the magic of mass production. One of the bars went to my friend's house and one stayed at mine. The other three we sold very easily through classified advertising like this: "*MUST SELL new $450.00 home bar, never used, ½ price.*"

Let's see how we came out on this deal. We each owned a bar valued at $450.00 if we had bought them at a retail store. From the sale of the other three we received $675.00; deducted the cost of the ad, $6.00, and the $250.00 I spent for the materials; leaving us with a grand total profit of $419.00 or $209.50 apiece. If you want to divide this amount by the number of hours we invested, you will find it to be about $12.30 an hour, working at home part-time. Not too bad, wouldn't you agree? Keep in mind our free bars in our own homes, so what was our time really worth? We did all of this and had our profit in our pocket less than three weeks from the time of materialization of the idea.

PROFITS FROM PICNIC TABLES

A week or so later, another friend of ours casually mentioned he was thinking about the purchase of a redwood picnic table and benches. At that time they were selling for about $60.00. We found the materials cost was about $16.00. (Today it's about double. Of course, retail is double also, so you can still come out well.) We asked our friend if he would buy the picnic table and benches from us if we could save him $20.00. He immediately agreed. Picnic tables and benches are constructed easily and quickly, so we made ten sets. It took us about twelve hours total. Here is how we disposed of the other nine:

We both had many old and useless-to-us items we wanted to dispose of, so we held a weekend garage sale and included our new picnic tables. All nine sold—six right in our own neighborhood.

Let's check the figures. The first one we sold for $40.00, the other nine sold for $42.50 each, for a total of $422.50 for the ten; subtract our $160.00 cost, and our profit was $262.50 or $131.25 each. Not quite as good as the bars, but still close to $11.00 an hour.

ADULT EDUCATION AND PROFIT POTENTIAL

Although we went into woodworking without any formal course of instruction, I'm still a firm advocate of spending a few hours receiving professional instruction in whatever you need to know. You will find it will be time well spent. I have taken adult education courses in macrame, pottery, leather craft, carpentry, household plumbing, and many other skills.

One course that turned a pretty penny for me was upholstering. I went to an adult education course that cost $12.00 for twelve hours, attended part-time and completed in two weeks. I made $400.00-plus out of this little deal.

I had an old, worn, unsightly couch that the Salvation Army should have hauled away, but I really didn't want to spend money for a new one. What to do? I called a furniture upholsterer and subsequently received a bid for $236.00 to recover that old junk-heap. Well, I didn't want to spend that kind of money. My financial condition had improved some by this time, but I could see no reason to start giving money away. This is when I signed up for the upholstery class. Well, I reupholstered that old couch myself; the cost was about $65.00 including renting a heavy-duty sewing machine. Friends and relatives raved and told other people. I eventually did several pieces of furniture for those other people. I averaged about $15.00 per hour for part-time work in my garage.

WANTED: USED CARS— REWARD OFFERED!

Here's a neat one with which I have made as much as $25.00 to $30.00 an hour. There is a big market for older used cars that look cared-for and that run well. People don't necessarily buy this type of car from a dealer; many times they will buy from an individual first. I'm talking about the $500.00 to $800.00 second car or starter car for a teen-ager. Most parents don't want a high-priced sooped-up car for their beginning drivers. When looking for that ten-year or older car, go to new and late model car dealers. When they take that car in on trade, they normally have little, if anything, invested in it and, therefore, wind up wholesaling it cheaply to a car lot that deals in older cars exclusively. If you're there first, you stand a good chance of buying that older car before a car lot. Following are some tips on buying older cars for making money:

1. Run a finger around inside tail pipe. If there's a heavy residue of oil, the car probably is an oil burner. Don't buy it.
2. Extreme inner or outer tire wear could indicate alignment problems, but in older cars probably serious and expensive front-end work. Also, check rear tires; they could have been switched.

3. If the engine has a miss, it could need simple tuning, but it could be an indication of burned or cracked valves, or even more serious mechanical problems. Have it checked by an impartial mechanic.
4. If the automatic transmission slips, check fluid level; if low, check for leaks; could be even more serious. Get expert advice from an impartial mechanic.
5. Avoid broken glass, ripped headliners, cracked padded dashes, ripped or torn upholstery panels in doors, bent bumpers and grills. They are all expensive to replace.
6. A ten-year-plus car will probably need paint, tires, seat covers and floor carpeting. That's fine. You can make money from it.

Here's what I did. I bought an eleven-year-old Chevy for $175.00 (the car dealer wanted $250.00—I offered $175.00); purchased used whitewall tires with good tread for $60.00, seat covers for $50.00 (easily self-installed), and carpet for $25.00 (also easily self-installed). Add a tune-up for $35.00 and a paint job for $70.00 at one of the national franchise quick-paint places; the total cost including car—$415.00. Then I licensed it. This is important. People like to buy a car if they think it's in use and not just sitting to be sold. It cost me $16.00 for the license. Then I took the car down to a service station that I gave all my business to, and asked the owner if I could park it there with a "For Sale" sign on it. Less than a week later it sold for $700.00. My profit was $269.00. My total time invested was nine hours, or—almost $30.00 per hour part-time. Other than installing seat covers and carpet, all I did was drive it to the various places to have others do the work on it. Incidentally, the nine hours included the time spent at car dealers trying to buy a car.

LUXURY ON A SHOESTRING

Most people do not know the model year of a car as long as it is late model and kept clean. In September of 1977, I started looking for a demo or a used car manufactured in 1977. My preference was a Thunderbird or Cordoba, as I knew there would be little or no major body change in 1978. This applied to Mark V, Cadillac, and many other cars.

On December 1, 1977, I found the perfect car and purchased it two days later. The black 1977 Thunderbird was loaded: power steering, brakes, windows and seats; air conditioning; AM/FM; tape deck; tilt steering wheel; cruise control; power door locks and trunk opener; special trim package; and, yes, even a power combination moon/sun roof. And, best of all, I paid only $6,000.00 for this $10,000.00 car.

How was I able to buy so much for so little? Very, very simply. Firstly, I bought a 1977 model after the 1978 versions were out. Secondly, my timing was good. I bought during snowy, dismal, cold weather when sales were slow and morale down. Thirdly, my new-looking used car had over 20,000 miles on it, normally a lot for a car less than one year old, but most of these were road miles and the car had had excellent care, looked beautiful, and ran perfectly as verified by two mechanics, who had checked it before I finalized the deal.) With the extended warranty I had absolutely no worries. Last but not least, I offered cash with no trade. Even if you do not have cash, you can offer cash by arranging your financing prior to purchase through your bank; your bank can even help you determine what to offer for a car through their automobile reports. In this case, I offered $200.00 below wholesale and it was accepted.

After finalizing the purchase I paid a total of $35.00 for the addition of four pieces of chrome and, eureka, I had a 1978 automobile. No one could tell the difference, including most car dealers. I enjoyed the prestige of driving my purchase a total of 43,000 trouble-free miles. I sold my 1977 Thunderbird at the end of July 1979, for $4,750.00—a cost of $1,250.00 over twenty months or $62.50 per month. (By the way, moon roof cars sell well in July.)

MY DEAL

Purchase Price	$6,000.00
Selling Price	4,750.00
Actual Cost	$1,250.00
Divided by 20 months	$ 62.50

MOST DEALS

Purchase Price	$10.000.00
Selling Price	4,750.00
Actual Cost	$ 5,250.00
Divided by 32 months	$ 164.06

As illustrated, many people pay much more to drive the same automobile than I did. The largest loss is in the first twelve months: $4,000 or $333.00 per month. Both figures are much higher than my $62.50 per month. The secrets are buy after the model year end instead of during or at the start of a model year; do not trade in a car, offer cash (arrange your own financing if necesary); time your purchase when car sales are slow; and sell when many people are looking for a better car (especially during summer for vacations).

3. *IN THE BEGINNING*

Essential ingredients for the science of **MMM** are all around us. Quite simply, **MMM** is the ability to *recognize* opportunity easily available and then to *assemble* that opportunity into a vehicle that will parlay itself to your best interest and advantage. In the following pages I will share with you not only my own experiences, but those of other people. You will find an assortment of ideas, business possibilities, and thought processes that can help actualize dreams of success. The only ingredients to add include yourself and your own ingenuity.

I have found it much easier to comply with and supply other people's needs and interests than to talk them into something I felt was needed and of interest. My insurance career is an illustration of this difference in approach. In the brainwashing training sessions conducted by the insurance company, they consistently alluded to the huge commission paid for each policy sold. Measuring the commission against the actual work, of writing the application and getting it processed to issuance, makes it seem possible that earnings could exceed the $200.00 per hour mark. But most people don't exactly beat a path to your door to buy life insurance. You are subjected to many negative reactions; old friends openly avoid you. Introduced to someone new, you are soon left standing by yourself while that new acquaintance dashes off to a just-remembered appointment. I finally determined that most people were not interested in buying more insurance. In fact, they were not interested even in talking about insurance. The company I worked for had a pat answer for this problem: "Situations like that should be considered a challenge and then turned to advantage through creative salesmanship." Frankly, friends, I find this life already poses many challenges, and it's not my intent to add more. Now let's continue on with the science of **MMM.**

CULTURED MARBLE MAGIC

Although not one of my projects, it directly pertains to opportunity of the moment and ingenuity. A few years back, one of my friends, let's call him Joe, overheard an acquaintance of his, let's call him Ralph, mention that he had been selected by his company to be the person responsible for arranging his company's Christmas banquet and employee gift program. Joe, in tune with money-making possibilities, seized upon this opportunity for a quick, easy profit. He asked Ralph if he would be interested in desk pen sets at a good price; as a $10.00 value for $6.00. Ralph was immediately intrigued and asked, "How soon could I see a sample of the desk sets?" Joe agreed to bring a sample to Ralph's home the next evening for his inspection and decision. Ralph was impressed and ordered eighty-two sets from Joe for delivery the following week. Joe delivered the desk pen sets for eighty-two employees and received a check for $492.00 of which $313.24 was profit for Joe. The company giving the gifts was happy, Ralph was happy he had saved his company money on gifts, and Joe was ecstatic.

It had taken a total of only twelve hours for him and his wife to produce the pen sets. That figures $26.10 per hour. They were able to do this in two evenings in their living room. I looked at the desk pen sets. They were absolutely beautiful, and yet unbelievably simple to make. Joe explained how he and his wife had learned to make desk pen sets. They had made it a custom to make gifts for members of the family, and over the years had made a variety of gift objects; just the year before they had made the desk pen sets as Christmas gifts for their families. Joe and his wife got the idea from shopping at a gift shop and discovering that some marble giftwares were not real marble at all, but a specially hardened and glazed form of plaster of Paris, just like the windowsills of their house. (Some newer homes have this type of sill instead of wood.) Joe checked a sill manufacturer and found the product called Cultured Marble. It could be cast in various forms at a very reasonable price. After considering several ideas for gift items, Joe and his wife decided on Cultured Marble desk pen sets as a family gift project, subsequently leading to a nice, easy, quick profit.

The pens and their holders were purchased from a manufacturer in Chicago they found through catalogues at a gift manufacturing supply company. Joe had Cultured Marble bases cast in several colors at $1.15 each, and ordered 164 desk pens with holders at 35¢ each (two pens with holders to a base). He drilled two holes in each of the Cultured Marble bases, attached the pens and holders, and covered the bottom of the bases with glued-on green felt (7¢ each). Then he attached a small brass plate (13¢ each) suitable for engraving making them look finished, professional, and expensive. They wrapped the sets in tissue paper and boxed them; with boxes purchased from a local box manufacturer, the packaging cost per gift was

13¢. Joe's cost on the desk pen sets, including packaging, was $2.18 each, which he sold to Ralph for $6.00 each.

I later lost track of Joe and his wife but would bet they continued to make money from recognizing opportunity.

USED PAPERBACK BOOKSELLER

Here's a real go-getter of an idea I wish I had tried, but by the time I heard about it I was already involved in many other projects.

Start going to garage sales and purchasing paperback books. You will probably find them priced at up to 50¢ each but, if you will buy out all that person has, you may get them as cheaply as 5¢ to 10¢ each. You should get a starting stock of 1,500 to 3,000 paperbacks which could cost you as little as $75.00 to $150.00. After collecting your stock, you can set up tables in your garage or basement. Categorize books into adventure, mystery, romance, science fiction, and other genres. Then pass the word to neighbors, friends, and relatives, that you are a used book dealer.

At today's prices for new paperbacks, you could easily charge 80¢ for one or $1.40 for two; or for people who want to trade, you could take in three of theirs for one of yours. You will still have plenty of cash business. Undoubtedly, while the traders are there they will also find something they want to buy.

Your business will increase if you do some advertising, but watch out, it could get too big. If you have too many cars parked by your curb at all hours, with people coming and going, officials could require you to rent a store if you wanted to continue business. This may be a good move. I know a fellow who owns a used paperback store in a shopping mall. All he does is run in twice a week, counts the money, makes his bank deposit, and then takes off to his other business. He says he clears about $1,800.00 a month after paying everything. That's not too bad for a small part-time job taking ten to sixteen hours a *month.*

HAVE BROOM, WILL TRAVEL

This could be a big winner for you, but it has one large drawback: you might actually have to *work* for a couple of weeks to learn something about the business, but after that you play while others work.

First of all, you should get a part-time job with some large janitorial company, maybe four hours a night, five or six days a week, for a few weeks. This should give you an adequate education in terms and general management plus an actual exposure to the working part of the business so that you can begin the second phase of this business. Your goal is to become a broker and leasor of janitorial businesses. I knew a man in a large city who was quietly getting rich doing just this.

The second phase will be lining up other business to use your janitorial service. This shouldn't be difficult once you explain precisely how you intend to handle your business, and how they can receive better, more reliable service through your methods. Explain that each one of your janitors is an independent businessman who has actually purchased his business under an independent contractor's agreement with you. Your janitors, as independent business people, exhibit greater reliability because they have an investment to protect. Presented this way, your method of operation will appeal to the businesses you are trying to secure as accounts. You can easily find out what they are paying for their present janitorial service simply by asking to see their contract agreement. From this contract you can establish exactly the present services and charges. If they are not under contract, ask them to tell you what they are paying and what is being done for them. Most businessmen have a pretty good idea what the cost of janitorial service should be.

You may miss on the first few contacts, but you will gain experience in bidding jobs. It is better to bid high—you can always come down—for if you bid too low it is difficult to come up. When you start accumulating clients interested in using your new-concept janitorial business, get definite commitments, such as signing a contract with you to start in thirty or sixty days and to run for one year, as long as they are satisfied with the service.

You will now be ready for the third phase. Using the classified job and business opportunity section of your local newspaper, you can advertise for people to do the actual janitorial work in this way: "*Wanted, people interested in having their own business. Solid, guaranteed income. Either part-time or full time. Very small equipment investment required. Easy terms available.*" Many other methods of advertising are possible. Experiment until one is right for you. As you select applicants who are sincere and ambitious, you simply rent them the business accounts that you have already set up on janitorial contracts. You could probably set it up so that you would collect all money, retain 20% and give them 80%, affording you control of the collections and service. With that split, your janitorial people will make much more money than if they worked for a commercial service.

Another angle to this business would involve supplying your janitorial people with equipment and supplies. This will further increase your profit and income by searching out appropriate jobbers and wholesalers in the equipment and chemical lines. You will be able to supply vacuum cleaners, floor polishers and buffers, mops, pails, brooms, and many other necessary items, plus cleaning chemicals of a wide variety, like window cleaners, soaps, deodorizers, and furniture polishes.

Many commercial janitorial companies pay only minimum wages to their employees, $3.00 to $4.00 per hour. Let's assume we have a small office complex that pays $300.00 per month for cleaning services. Let's further assume that cleaning requires two hours per night, five nights a week or twenty nights per month. Compare your operation and JXY Janitorial Company.

YOUR COMPANY		**JXY COMPANY**	
Account pays per month	**$300.00**	Account pays per month	**$300.00**
Your contract janitor works 20 nights for 2 hours @80% of billing	**$240.00**	Co. employee is paid 20 nights for 2 hours per night @$3.00	**$120.00**
Your net profit (and you supply (nothing)	**$ 60.00**	Company profit (they pay for all machines, supplies, trucks and many other things)	**$180.00**

JXY's profit looks good until you start deducting all that they pay out for equipment, supplies, transportation, administration, management, training, and so on. What *you* have left is net—your actual income. Of course, you do pay income tax on your earnings as everyone else does.

Now, let's again assume some additional hypothetical figures based on your signing fifty $300.00-a-month accounts and supplying the contract janitors to service them.

YOUR NET FOR EACH ACCOUNT = $60.00
$300.00 - $240.00 = $60.00 X 50 = $3,000.00

Three thousand dollars per month, $36,000.00 per year—not a bad annual income; and then, if you add your profits for supplying equipment and supplies, it might easily amount to another $5,000.00 and up. The beautiful part is that this $41,000.00-a-year business could be operated right out of your home.

SOME GOOD TIPS FOR SUCCESSFUL OPERATION

A. Select only ambitious, industrious, sincere applicants for contract janitors (husband-and-wife teams are good).

B. Require applicants to make a cash investment covering their cost of equipment and supplies. (If they have no cash available, but have good credit rating, perhaps a bank will lend them money, or maybe you could arrange for them to put it on a charge account.)

C. Be precise in your bookkeeping. Have an attorney draw up your independent contractor agreements. (Be sure to include a noncompete clause for several years' duraation. This protects your accounts from cannibalization by an unethical contract janitor.) Also, confer with a C.P.A. for maximum profit structures.

You should be able to set up the mechanics of this business and begin earning income within sixty days or less, depending on your organizational ability and desire.

This business can earn both you and your contract janitors handsome incomes for years to come. The exciting part is starting with little or no investment of your own.

I am going to leave the additional, expanded or replacement earnings (better known as income multiplication) portion of **MMM** temporarily in order to outline ways of saving money (referred to as creative purchasing), which is an important segment of **MMM.** We shall be returning to ways and ideas concerning earnings in the final chapters of this book. There you will find many more money ideas that will help you attain the position of *Armchair Millionaire.*

4. IMPROVING SAVINGS

Early in 1976 my life was zipping along pretty well between my full-time job and my part-time, moneymaking ventures. I was doing fine but the restlessness concerning my financial destiny was still nagging me. I wasn't particularly interested in taking on additional money-building ventures. I was having a good time in leisure hours, and felt I had earned my fun. I decided to further review my spending habits and see if I could make them more efficient.

The following pages will give you a concise report of what my investigations revealed in regard to saving money out of the funds I was already spending without sacrificing any aspect of my lifestyle. I repeat, "Money saving is also of prime consideration and importance in the implementation of the **MMM** science."

LIFE INSURANCE

About this time I began to see many articles about whole life insurance as opposed to term insurance and annuities. These articles were written by well-known economists, columnists, government officials, and even recognized insurance professionals. With my brief insurance background, I decided to see what savings were available in this area, and wound up with some astounding facts. Whole life insurance was only producing in cash values at age sixty-five as low as one-fifth of what term insurance and annuities could produce at the same age. Check the charted comparison.

Sample Illustration

Whole Life Paid at 65
Age 20 - Annual Premium $90.35

Year	Insurance		Cash Value (Ins.)
1	$5,000.00	*OR*	$ 2.15
20	$5,000.00	*OR*	$1,417.95
40	$5,000.00	*OR*	$3,146.20
45	$5,000.00	*OR*	$3,699.50

At age 65 $5,000.00 paid up insurance *or* cash value of $3,699.50 or $20.53 per month 10 years certain.
Note: A copy of this particular policy is currently in my files.

Sample Illustration

Term Plus 7½% Annuity
Age 20 - Annual Cost $90.35

Year	Insurance		Cash Value (Inv.)
1	$5,000.00	*PLUS*	$ 62.85
20	$5,000.00	*PLUS*	$ 2,673,42
28	*OPTIONAL	*PLUS*	$ 5,239.57
40	OPTIONAL	*PLUS*	$14,143.55
45	OPTIONAL	*PLUS*	$20,829.64

*It came to my attention that you could drop your insurance in the 28th year because the annuity value was already higher than the face amount of the insurance.
At age 65 optional insurance, Cash Value or $173.58 per month 10 years certain.
Note: Significant difference between the two illustrations is insurance or cash value and greater all cash value.

If you have larger amounts of insurance and premium than shown, just multiply all figures by an amount close to what you have. This will give you a rough estimate. (Example: If you have $25,000.00, multiply all figures in the illustration by five.) At this point, if you were you, I would contact my insurance agent for a full explanation. Also, it would not hurt to contact some other agents and get full quotas of costs on term insurance and annuities. In my case, I did not buy an annuity. I cut my basic insurance cost by 65% and put what cash values I had into things that at least keep pace with inflation's current rates. In comparison, the insurance companies' 2½–4% interest figures on some of the older policies did not even come close.

This is not an indictment of the insurance industry. The important point in selecting an insurance agent is making sure he or she is an educated professional with your best interests in mind. (You will see how to do this in a later chapter dealing with the Five-Deep Selection Process.) The proper kind of insurance and financial or estate planning is a valuable asset to any family regardless of income, but all too often we find ourselves dealing with a greenhorn from some distant insurance company. Little or no direct supervision is provided, and that same inexperienced agent may well consider the amount of his commission long before he considers your true insurance need. My advice is know your agent and the company he represents.

DISTRIBUTORSHIP BUYING

While searching for money-saving avenues, I was reading income and business opportunity magazines for additional ideas, and a new thought surfaced. The total membership of my family was quite large, which meant through the course of a year many birthday, anniversary, wedding, Christmas, and a general multitude of other gifts. In reading the magazines, I had noticed a score of advertisements concerning distributorships of all kinds of merchandise, all the way from jewelry, cosmetics, and clothing, to what-have-you. My first reaction was that they were probably come-ons, actually costing retail-plus, but I wrote for additional information anyway.

Much to my amazement and delight I found that a large share of the offers were legitimate and you actually could buy many items at wholesale prices if you became a distributor. This opened new vistas for me. I wrote for more distributorship information on anything that happened to hit my fancy. I thoroughly investigated their price offerings, comparing with similar items at department stores. My files began to fill up with information and offers of all types of merchandise. I must have been put on a national mailing list, because information began to arrive from companies with which I had no correspondence. Finally I selected several companies that interested me most and became a distributor with them. Some charged me for becoming a distributor, for some I became a distributor simply by purchasing a few samples, and others were entirely free—I just signed an agreement. Many of the items were 30–50% and more off for distributors.

My first year I saved and made over $1,300.00, between saving on gift purchases and things for my own use and selling a few things to friends who begged me for them. I saved over $250.00 on my Christmas shopping alone. The old saying, "A penny saved is a penny earned," developed great significance for me. Think what would happen if our government, at both state and federal levels, would adopt a money-saving policy. In a very short time we could forget about runaway, double-digit inflation. We, the people, or the American buying public, have let ourselves be guided into becoming a herd of impulse purchasers. I was one for many years. The Madison Avenue advertisers put long hours into creating ads to separate you from your money quickly and efficiently, and will continue to do so as long as you allow. They continually produce advertising of shiny new automobiles, luxurious furniture, and literally thousands of other items psychologically engineered to get you to do one thing—*buy, buy, buy.* They would rather you not take any time to think about your purchases. If you did, it might drastically cut down on the amount of money that eventually finds its way into their pockets.

I want to share an experience that happened to me a couple of years ago. At the time, there was a certain type of extremely sophisticated television set that was all the huge rage, very expensive, with all the gadgets to make it more desirable. I really wanted one in the worst way, but I dug in my heels and resisted. Instead I started watching the classified ads in the newspaper and, sure enough, not ninety days later I saw one advertised by a private party. These people were typically the sort of impulse buyers that the national advertisers prey upon. They had bought, bought, bought—until they wound up in such a hole that they could not pay for all of their purchases. This created money problems and general dissent in their marriage. They had decided to split up and sell everything, I suppose in an effort to get even and start fresh. The television set was in immaculate condition, worked perfectly, still under warranty. They had traded in their old television plus some cash, and therefore only owed about half what the television had originally sold for (plus, of course, over 20% annual interest; they had financed the balance of their purchase). What they wanted was someone to take over their monthly payments and relieve them of the obligation.

Well, I had generated surplus cash through my moneymaking, money-saving ventures, and was in a position to pay off the finance company, thereby saving that exorbitant amount of interest. Everyone was happy: the couple was released from financial obligations; the finance company reduced a liability that could have turned into a repossession and charge-off; and I saved 50% of the initial purchase price.

Many years ago my father had a favorite saying: "What you earn is not near as important as what you do with what you earn." When I was younger I didn't necessarily feel that my old dad could be considered exactly a fountain of wisdom. How many of us have been guilty of that shortcoming? The older I became the smarter my dad became, in my eyes. It *does* pay to listen to the experience of others. I have duplicated the savings of the television set in many things that I have purchased. This is known as creative purchasing, or getting double mileage out of your earnings. The only thing needed is the patience to wait for what you want to come along, at a price you are willing to pay, within reason, of course. Don't expect to pay $50.00 for a new $1,000.00 item. People may get hard-pressed, but they don't get stupid. A reasonable expectation is to pay 50–60% of the original price for something almost new. If you make a habit of watching going-out-of-business, stock reduction and clearance sales, you may buy something still in the crate, so to speak, at 50% of stated retail. Don't be afraid to make an offer, even if something is already marked with a price. I have done this in several instances, and walked away with the item at my price.

Grocery costs are something you will have a hard time saving 40% on, unless you own a grocery store, but you can effectively save 10–15% through wiser purchasing. (There is a sixty-five-page booklet available from The Better Shopper Kit. One of the developers of this kit is Cornell University's Heinz Biesdorf, who has earned the sobriquet of the Penny-Pinching Professor. The information on obtaining this kit is found on the last pages of this book.) Meat, fowl, and fresh vegetables are entirely another matter. Let me tell you what I did with those items. I went outside of town a short distance, and made a deal with a farmer. I bought two beef calves, gave him one, and let him graze mine with the rest of his herd. I started the same system with chickens, except I bought a hundred, gave him fifty and I kept fifty. The end result was that I was paying about half for my meat. This included any extra feeding, butchering, and packaging.

I am a firm advocate of increasing income or saving money by methods that do not require any major additional time. Now let me tell you how I managed a fresh vegetable garden with a minimum amount of work on my part. I had a large corner lot with too much grass in the backyard, requiring many hours of maintenance. One Saturday morning, bright and early, I rented a rototiller and tore up over half of that large backyard with the help of a neighborhood couple who had a yard too small for a garden. By five o'clock we had it all planted with a variety of popular vegetables. My deal with the other couple was this: I supplied the ground and rented the rototiller, and they helped plant, and we split the cost of plants and seed. They used my water and did the actual physical labor of irrigating and keeping the garden weeded until it was all harvested. We evenly split the total produce of the garden. Everything went according to plan, and the only actual work I put in was one Saturday's labor that I would have spent anyway just cutting the grass in that old backyard. You may wonder about the cost of irrigating the garden—well, I thought of that, too. I probably would have used about the same amount of water just maintaining the half a backyard that I converted into garden area. I had good, fresh vegetables at a fraction of the cost I would have paid in a grocery store. I even made a deal with a lady to can some of them for me by letting her keep half of what she canned.

Once you establish a money-saving pattern, a chain reaction seems to materialize. This was also true of my moneymaking ventures. You can become more and more creative. At one point, several of my friends accused me of having the so-called Midas touch. I am sure no one really has that touch, but everyone can develop the magic of the **MMM** process. Later on in this book I will tell you how I bought a house through using **MMM**; also how my wife and I opened our own small business out of our basement ($80.00 investment.) A business, I might add, that was capable of earning us $10,000.00 per month. You will see how we obtained office furniture when needed without spending any of our money for it. As you continue to read the balance of this book, let your thoughts have free rein. I'm sure you are already identifying with many of the circumstances I found myself in. Think about it. There really is a solution for every problem.

5. COMPARING APPROACHES

Let's establish a hypothetical comparison of two people—Paul and Bob. Paul uses the creative purchase portion of the science of **MMM**, while Bob does not. Both earn $20,000.00 per year, and will continue to do so for the next ten years. From these salaries we will deduct the cost of housing payment, lights, gas, water, and telephone. Four hundred per month adds up to $4,800.00 per year. Deducting that amount from $20,000.00 per year gross income leaves $15,200.00, which will be spent on general living costs.

Both of these people enjoy equal lifestyles, but here is where the similarity ends and a great difference begins. As previously stated, Paul uses **MMM**, Bob does not. Paul pays only 60% on the average for the same item both he and Bob purchase, thereby creating a 40% overall savings for Paul. Reducing this to actual savings in dollars and cents, it means Paul is enjoying the same lifestyle as Bob for 60% of his $15,200.00, or effectively creating savings in the amount of $6,080.00 per year. If Paul were to do nothing more than deposit his savings in a good tax deferred annuity paying only 9% over the next ten years, his total accumulation, including interest, would be a staggering $100,033.00.

Let's go another ten years predicated on the same formula; this sum would then grow to $399,904.00. We could assume Paul was thirty years old when he started using **MMM**, and continued until age sixty-two; at which time, Paul's savings would total $1,081,000.00! Amazing, isn't it? And what has Bob done in this time? Nothing. And what has Bob accumulated? Again, nothing. Oh, perhaps an equity in his home, of course, which Paul also has. But who would you rather be, Paul or Bob?

Now we will discuss a third person by the name of Tom. He used **MMM** also, but he was more adventurous than Paul. He also applied the other half of **MMM**, which is creating expanded earnings with income multiplication in the form of business opportunities, thereby doubling or tripling Paul's best efforts, for a whopping final figure of $2,174,000.00 to $3,261,000.00.

The full range of **MMM** includes money-saving and money-earning devices; a beginner might consider distributorships with Amway or Shaklee. For the nominal cost of a distributorship you can begin saving up to 30% and more on many items that you are including in your grocery shopping, such as soaps, deodorants, and all types of cleaners; in fact, between the two, almost any household item is available. Add to this list a variety of vitamins, and even some gift and jewelry lines; and to fully round out a distributor line, Amway even has a catalogue offering all sorts of general merchandise—televisions, clothes, tools, and a multitude of other items. I have used many Amway and Shaklee products, and have found them to be high quality, in my opinion, totally cost-efficient and competitive with retail brands. I have heard some people say, "They cost too much." I have not found this to be true. It is a fact that, because of their highly concentrated forms, each container may seem to cost more, but if you will use them exactly according to directions, I think you may determine, as I have, they are actually a bit cheaper. You may suspect that I am presently receiving a gratuity from the two companies just mentioned—not so. I just feel that they provide one way for the **MMM** novice to begin not only money-savings, but money-earnings, as soon as today.

One couple with a large family had been buying Amway products introduced to them by a relative, and became great believers of the products. They finally determined they were spending about $1,800.00 a year in buying Amway merchandise. (I questioned this figure as it sounded high to me, but they proved it. Afterward, I checked with other peole to see how much they were spending at the local grocery store buying products that they could buy from Amway, and thereafter, judged that the couple was probably entirely correct. You might take a look at your own purchases.) The couple decided to become distributors themselves in order to save approximately 30% on their purchases. Thirty percent of $1,800.00 is $540.00 per year. They told me, after obtaining their distributorship, they began buying more of their needed items from Amway, including gifts and even large items. At the time I talked to them, they sincerely believed they were saving $200.00 a month just by virtue of being distributors. I concur that this is totally possible.

Before adding this section to my book, I decided that I should make a more thorough investigation of these savings allegations. Here is what I turned up. Many distributors of these products actually are saving $25.00,

$50.00, and even up to $300.00 a month in their personal purchases; in addition, they are retailing merchandise for extra money, signing up other distributors for more earnings, and enjoying a tax savings by running a business out of their homes.

6. *BUYING REAL ESTATE*

In September 1976, using **MMM** my wife and I decided we wanted a home more suitable for a basement business and after a short search we found the perfect home. The two-story house had a full basement, two-car garage, four bedrooms, 2½ baths, formal dining room, family room with fireplace, slate floor formal foyer, large lot, landscaping, and a six-foot cedar fence. It was in a good neighborhood, close to schools, churches, and shopping, plus close to a country club which we later joined. The place was available at a price and terms we could very easily afford, but we did not let the sellers know this. (When using **MMM** it is better not to divulge your financial abilities and bargaining power until you learn a few things about the sellers of whatever you are buying.)

In the course of conversation with the sellers we found they were very motivated, almost desperate to sell because of financial reverses. Their income was way down. The husband had been offered a good job in another state, which required an immediate move. Because of diminishing savings and lack of income, making payments was very difficult. In fact, they had borrowed money on a second mortgage to keep everything going, which just added to their financial burdens. Incidentally, on the second mortgage the bank not only had taken it on their house, but had included office furniture and equipment that the sellers owned. The house was in need of a little paint here and there, some minor cleanup, getting the yard back in shape, tree and bush trimming, etc. We accomplished it all in three or four weekends. The point is that the house did not show as well as it should.

The sellers had the home priced at $49,500.00, which was a couple thousand dollars under market value already, but they were very concerned that the house might go another sixty or ninety days without selling, and they were already late with their payments. We told the sellers we would think it over for three or four hours and get back to them. Four and one-half hours later we called them and said, "We have been thinking about your house. It is a little more than we were prepared to pay, but with some careful management we could handle it. We have been trying to think of a way to give you cash and assume your loans. We know that would help your situation, whereas if we went with a new loan we would be looking at a minimum of perhaps up to sixty days. We know that you are saving a realtor's fee by trying to sell your house yourselves, but most people, including ourselves, do not feel comfortable without the advice of a competent realtor. However, if we could submit an offer subject to the approval of our attorney, I think we would be inclined to deal directly with you. We will see how much available cash we can come up with and drop by at seven-thirty this evening to discuss it." In this conversation I established several important points. One, we had limited cash. Two, they could be looking at another sixty days to get the house closed and moved, plus being further behind in a financial situation they already could not afford. Three, though most people would be most comfortable dealing with a realtor, it would cost them around 7% and further delay.

The stage was set and we appeared on their doorstep at ten minutes of eight. (Timing is critical. Don't appear too anxious. We were late on both our phone call and personal appearance without any explanation.) We told the sellers, after reviewing our cash-available situation, we felt we had a solution for everybody. One, we wanted the home in present condition. Two, we needed the office furniture listed on the second deed of trust, therefore, they would not have to move it out of the basement where it was stored. I pointed out that even though the furniture had cost three or four thousand dollars and was in nice shape, it would probably take time to sell and move, and they would realize only fifty or sixty cents on the dollar; if they called an office furniture liquidator he would probably give them twenty or thirty cents on the dollar. The bank might not be happy with part of the security being sold, and could demand an immediate payoff of the second mortgage.

Here was our proposition: we would buy the house, keep the office furniture, assume both the first and second loans (both had good interest rates), give them $3,000.00 in cash, and they could move as soon as they wanted. They snapped our offer up. We closed on the house and moved in, all within ten days. We had succeeded in impressing them with all the problems and delays they could be facing. We bought our new piece of real estate for $41,500.00, simply by assuming two loans. We consider our $3,000.00 went for office furniture, in which we planned to invest that much anyway. Twenty-three months later we sold that moneymaker for $67,500.00 after costs. That left a cool net to us of $26,000.00, or you might say we made $1,313.00 per month additional for living expenses and being able to conduct our business from that house. We still have the office furniture and use it daily.

You can see why the seller snapped up our offer and how we made a tremendous deal for ourselves.

Home Value	$51.500.00 (+)
Condition and Appearance	2,000.00 (-)
Realtors Fee if Listed at 7%	3,605.00 (-)
Seller Making Payments 60, Maybe even 90 Days	1,200.00 (-)
Continued Loss of Income 60-90 Days	4,500.00 (-)
Sale of Office Furniture	1,200.00 (+)
Grand Total	$41.395.00

As you can see, the seller had an actual value of only $41,395.00. We paid $41,500.00. He actually made a profit of $105.00 from our purchase, and did not have to gamble. It is true he may have won and come out with more cash by waiting for another buyer, but he could have lost; perhaps his good job opportunity would not have waited. Many things could have happened.

Our deal was fair to everyone. You do not have to gouge and cheat people in order to make large sums of money. You *do* have to be a conscientious, cautious buyer so that you do not become the one gouged or cheated. I have made very good money out of real estate, some directly with a seller, or buyer, some through a realtor, but always with **MMM**, using one of its essential ingredients —creative purchasing.

7. HOME BUSINESS

Alex and Carla did not seem to be the type of people whom you would immediately associate with the world of door-to-door direct selling. Alex had been a schoolteacher for fifteen years; Carla, a mother and housewife for the last twelve. But after hearing their business plan, I had to conclude it was excellent and made good sense.

RECIPE FOR SUCCESS

In order to promote their neighborhood business, they devised a way to make it easy, friendly, and totally devoid of direct sales pressure. Carla was an excellent cook and had developed a hobby of collecting recipes. Over the years she accumulated in excess of two thousand recipes.

This hobby of hers became an integral part of their sales plan. They developed a monthly neighborhood one-page newsletter containing a new recipe, helpful household hints, and neighborhood news, such as baby-sitting services, marriages, graduations, etc. Alex was the newsletter's editor and Carla its typist. They then took it to a local fast-copy service for duplication ($12.00 per month).

With these copies in hand, Carla made her way

through their general neighborhood, covering about four hundred homes. She explained that they planned to deliver the newsletter each month thereafter, and it would contain a new recipe and information pertaining to the neighborhood. Further she explained that they were also new distributors of Amway products. (This could apply to any of the other distributors.) Because of the free recipe and newsletter approach, people did not become hostile when she knocked at their door. Instead she was greeted warmly and with interest, particularly when she let it be known she was also a neighborhood resident.

Carla learned an interesting thing. Some of the people in her area had been purchasers of Amway products and had liked them, but were no longer being serviced because of losing track of the distributor. Carla made some immediate sales. This came as an unexpected, pleasant surprise to Alex and Carla. They had felt that the first sales would happen after delivery of the second newsletter and contact. Incidentally, their plan called for dropping off catalogues to the more interested customers with the delivery of the second newsletter.

Their program involved delivering four hundred newsletters monthly, then developing 25% of the readers into Amway purchasers, who would spend a low average of $30.00 per month on Amway items. They would accomplish this because of three basic reasons. Firstly, they were building good public relations through their newsletter. Secondly, Alex and Carla were residents of the same general area; they were handy if someone ran out of something and needed it immediately. Thirdly, the quality and wide variety of merchandise would sell itself through word-of-mouth within their area.

I see nothing wrong with these assumptions. They make good, solid business sense. After all, Avon, Fuller Brush, and others have been making money year after year through neighborhood sales. Alex's projection of 25%, or one hundred families, averaging $30.00 a month in purchases means $3,000.00 in gross sales, of which approximately 30% was their profit. Just using the 30% figure makes their home business income about $900.00 per month. Including the savings on the purchases made by the family, estimated at $200.00 per month, makes the distributorship worth $1,100.00 per month to them. Alex and Carla felt that after they had delivered the newsletter for a few months themselves, they would be set firmly enough with their customers to hire a couple of area teen-age students to deliver the newsletter for a nominal fee. When this was accomplished Alex felt that he and Carla would be putting in only forty hours a month, shared between them, to maintain the $900.00-a-month profit level—$22.50 an hour from a part-time home business.

GOLD JOURNALISM

Thinking about Alex and Carla's newsletter made me remember another terrific little home business along the same lines, but on a larger scale. The fellow who started it was pretty ingenious. He had no money to start anything, but fortunately did possess a lot of sheer determination. He lived in a town of over 200,000 people. The resort-type town attracted a certain amount of tourism and, therefore, had an abundance of motels, restaurants, and entertainment establishments.

This enterprising entrepreneur, without any experience in journalism or the newspaper business, decided to go into the publishing and advertising business—not as an employee, but as the publisher of his own restaurant and entertainment guide. And here is how he put it together: first, he contacted restaurants, theaters, entertainment centers, and tourist attractions with his idea. He would sell them display advertising space in his publication at about half of what they were paying the daily newspapers. To top it off, he published only once a week. Therefore, the public would see the advertisement for a full seven days instead of just one. (Daily newspapers are generally read the day they are published, then hit the trash basket.) He would then distribute his publication free to motels, gas stations, grocery stores, and other key places. Some smooth thinking here. After giving it some thought in regards to readership, I realized that tourists who have been traveling usually would arrange a motel room or gas-up the car before taking in the sights. Therefore, those two businesses could supply their patrons with valuable information in the form of a publication that cost them nothing. The publication was a public relations boon to motels and gas stations. And, of course, the restaurants, entertainment centers and tourist attractions were profiting from their paid advertising.

The angle that stumped me was delivering his publication to grocery stores, since tourists don't often patronize supermarkets while on vacation. But a paper with just business display advertising promoting tourism does not reach the general residency of a town; therefore, he included public announcements at no charge, and classified want ads at about half the cost at a daily newspaper. And what better place to have people pick up his publication than their local supermarket? The supermarket was providing customers with an additional free service.

The publisher was taking in about $2,800.00 to $3,000.00 per week from the charges to advertisers. A local company printed 10,000 copies at $700.00. A local art service did the advertisements, typing, layout and design—$900.00. His wife was his secretary, his home his office, and he did all the advertising sales. Now, you may have already put your pencils to the figures and found out what his income and weekly profit is, but in case you haven't, it is $1,200.00 to $1,400.00 per week. The nice part is that he has most of his advertisers under long-term contracts.

FREE-LANCE LOAN BROKER

Here is a moneymaker started on an $80.00 investment, capable of producing over $100,000.00 a year in income, and successfully worked from a home basement. I can attest to all of these facts, because it was *my* moneymaker. Late 1975 my financial picture had improved enough through moneymaking, money-saving ventures that, once again, I felt confined by my guaranteed income job. Only *this* time I had a plan I knew would succeed. Business opportunity magazines carried numerous advertisements urging readers to become home mortgage and loan brokers, arranging loans for people in the process of buying homes. There was quite a lot of paperwork involved, but none of it overly difficult. The only hitch I could see was dealing with out-of-town or state lending institutions. This could create delays which would make buyers, sellers, or realtors unhappy with my service. I reasoned if there were out-of-town or state lending institutions willing to do this, undoubtedly there were local companies also willing. Because of my correspondence with the out-of-town and state companies, I was well armed with information, commission scales offered, and ideas on how to set myself up as a mortgage loan broker or banker. I contacted a total of two local lending institutions before making a deal with one. This required about two hours of my time and I was well on my way to what was to bcome a very lucrative, easy business. My responsibilities included contacting realtors to drum up business with their customers, then taking a preliminary loan application, ordering a credit report, and obtaining job verifications and any other information directly pertaining to requirements necessary for loan approval or rejection. After receiving all the necessary documentation, I submitted a penciled rough draft of the final loan application to the lending institution. The office typed the completed loan application and submitted it through the proper channels, such as VA, FHA, or conventional loan committees. When the loan was closed I received my fee—1% of the loan amount. My average loan was around $40,000.00, therefore, my earnings averaged $400.00. Total work time for each loan was approximately three and one-half hours, amounting to earnings of $114.29 per hour. See why I said lucrative?

You might wonder why a lending institution would make this kind of deal and pay what appears to be an exorbitant amount of money for the service. But consider that the company had no obligation to me, such as guaranteed salary, expense account, or employee benefits, like company car, insurances, employee compensations, vacation pay, office space, etc. The company's only obligation was to pay me 1% on every loan I produced, and then *only* if I produced loans. So there was no gamble on their part. The lending institution I dealt with trained me, a matter of four part-time days. Later, I trained my wife and she joined me in this highly profitable business. We have handled as many as twenty-six loans in one month. Our lowest month was five, but I spent that entire month in the hospital. The last five months we spent in this business, in addition to other interests, we averaged fifteen loans a month. Our income from the mortgage loan business was running $6,000.00 per month and we were working only twenty-two to twenty-eight hours a week from our basement.

Note: When I started into this business I retained my salaried job for about sixty days, at which time I was earning more part-time in two weeks than what my salaried job was paying me in a month. I recommend this procedure if you would rather not gamble. There are many types of home or part-time business you can overlap with full-time commitments.

DOUGH FROM DOUGH

Here's a little gem I learned about from a widow with two elementary school-aged children to support. She did not want a standard eight-to-five job which would leave her children unattended for about an hour in the morning and three hours in the afternoon. If she hired a baby-sitter for this amount of time it would overload her meager salary. Having been a homemaker and mother for several years prior to her husband's death, she was finding it difficult to enter the job market at anything above a trainee's earnings. With a small amount of savings left, she decided to start her own home business. She bought a small used donut-maker and added to her baking and cookie-making equipment. To promote her business, she went out to other businesses, car dealerships, insurance and real estate offices, large office complexes, factories—

wherever people might be interested in cookies, donuts, or cakes for sales meetings, morning coffee breaks, and so on. Because she offered to deliver and supply fresh baked goods, it didn't take her very long to establish a regular route. She was able to make her deliveries after the children went to school. Soon she hired a neighborhood lady to make deliveries for her. Shortly thereafter, she expanded her home business to making special occasion and custom wedding cakes. She told me that she was earning twice as much as an experienced secretary, working fewer hours, and able to be home when her children were.

HI-HO SILVER!

Being a gentleman rancher myself, I was especially intrigued with this idea. This would be a terrific way to make money if you own or have access to some good pastureland and water within a reasonable commuting distance to a fairly large town. I may try this one myself for a while. After once getting it organized, I can see how a person might make $1,500.00 a month and work only three or four hours in the entire month, and that would just be paperwork.

This individual started his business by purchasing fifteen Welsh and Shetland ponies. (I wasn't aware ponies were as cheap as they are. Less than $100.00 will buy a good one.) He then bought used pony saddles and bridles cheaply, and a used horse trailer that would transport up to ten ponies. So while ten ponies worked, the other five rested in the pasture. He then had a welder build him a pony walker, which looks like a big wheel with ten spokes. You harness the ponies to the spokes, and they walk in a circle so you have them under control.

He then contacted a large car dealership with a proposition. He would rent them the entire pony ride, complete with supervisor, for one month, as a public relations and advertising gimmick. His charge for the one month: $3,000.00. The time, no Sundays or Mondays; Tuesday through Friday 3:30 to 8:30 P.M., Saturday 9:00 A.M. to 7:00 P.M. The car dealer jumped at the opportunity! Why? The pony ride was offered during prime time when kids were out of school. The pony ride was free. Small kids have to get their parents to drive them to something like that. While kids were on the ponies, it was only natural that the parents would take a look at new cars, if they just happened to be sitting close by, and if there just happened to be sharp salespeople close by. You guessed it—sales zoomed. It proved to be a very successful promotion, far better than spending the money in newspaper advertising. (Did you know that full page ads may cost from $600.00 to $1,000.00 and more? And you may see the same car dealer run two or three a week.) It is reported that the owner of the pony ride has a waiting list of car dealers, furniture stores, shopping malls, etc. Now here's my idea of how to make $1,500.00 a month for three or four hours' work. For perhaps $700.00 a month, you could hire a person who handles horses to be the supervisor and to transport the ponies from the pasture to the pony ride. Eight hundred a month would take care of equipment payments, gasoline, wear and tear on equipment (truck, horse trailer, walker), insurance, and feeding and quartering ponies. This would leave you $1,500.00 a month for answering inquiries and scheduling your ride. If you really want to think big, how about ten such rides—$15,000.00 per month. Of course, then you would have to work probably thirty or forty hours a month.

MONEY TREES

This idea grabbed my attention in a hurry for several reasons. It is novel, easy, profitable, and can be as small or as large as you want to go. It could be started on almost zero capital if you're willing to go slow and just let it build, or you could invest significant funds (even borrowed), and enjoy returns directly proportionate to your investment, ability, and desire.

We will refer to our principal as Sally. Through family hardships, and no fault of her own, Sally was forced to drop out of high school at the end of her sophomore year and seek steady full-time employment to help her family. Her mother and father were victims of a serious automobile accident which left them handicapped for life. The same accident was responsible for the death of a younger sister and, for a while, the only income was what Sally could earn. Because of her limited education, jobs were menial and salary meager. Yet it was one of the menial jobs that launched Sally on a business career of her own. Today she is highly successful, employs several other people, and is a respected businesswoman in the community. Her business: renting or leasing trees and plants to area businesses. Sally still says she got into business by accident, but I think she took advantage of an opportunity that presented itself, teaming it with her own ambition and desire for a fulfillment of success. Her venture began when she accidentally overheard her then-boss complain about having to water and take care of the plants in the office, and how he was tired of seeing the same old plants year after year. On hearing this, Sally began to develop an idea. In the small home that she shared with her parents there were some forty or fifty house plants of various sizes and types since Sally had a way with plants. That afternoon she made an offer to her bosses. She volunteered to take over the complete care of the office plants, to include watering, general care, and even trading some of theirs for some of hers. She further agreed to let her bosses pay whatever they felt this service was worth. You can imagine Sally's delight when the following month her pay increased by $20.00, particularly when she measured her time involved against her raise in pay. The total time expended was a little over three hours, or broken down hourly, close to $6.66 an hour, almost three times her regular earnings. Sally started contacting other business places during her lunch hour, after work, or on Saturdays. She was both surprised and happy with startling results within a short period of time. She was matching her full-time income with her part-time business income in only about fourteen hours a week. A new business and career had begun. Today Sally is happily married. Her husband, Dan, is an enthusiastic partner in their flourishing business and they employ both of Sally's parents. They design and manufacture their own macrame and pots for use in business and resale; they own a separate retail plant store; they drive expensive cars, live in a prestigious home, and completely enjoy life. This, I think you will agree, is in the finest tradition of **MMM**.

Here are some ideas for starting your own plant leasing and rental business:

1. You can buy young plants cheaply, or start your own from shoots of older plants. The secret is to have a large variety of attractive adult plants when you start commercially. Forty or fifty should do.
2. If you are artistic and talented, make your own macrame, redecorate old pots purchased at flea

markets, garage sales, Salvation Army, etc. This will save you loads of money in start-up capital.

3. Plants take little space—an unused corner or bedroom would do as long as it opens to good sunlight. I know one lady who has in excess of 150 plants, all grouped around a living room window.
4. Plant-raising is easy, but I do suggest you buy some books pertaining to some of the more sophisticated methods if you are not entirely confident.
5. Using your home to raise and rent plants can be very enjoyable and profitable. Also, you can realize a significant tax break by allocation of a specified area within your home for this business; secure the services of a good bookkeeping and tax firm before applying the tax break—they can set it up the right way. (You might also be able to rent them plants—every business can be a prospect.)
6. Prices for the rental and service seem to vary. One plant rental operation charges $20.00 per month for four medium-sized plants, pots, and hanger. Service and watering require less than one hour per month. They rotate the plants about every six months, either back into their own stock or to another business place. They are handling around 100 accounts monthly. This develops about $2,000.00 in income monthly. They service their accounts in about twenty hours per week. That breaks down to about $25.00 per hour. Of course, this couple is very experienced and their accounts are closely grouped. Experiment with prices and hours.

7. If you are extremely confident and adventurous, this is a business you could possibly borrow money for and go into in a big way. But one word of caution: set up accounts under a tentative rental agreement first.
8. Why would a business rent plants from you? It benefits from the beauty of plants rotated regularly, with no responsibility for maintenance, and is eligible for 100% tax deduction.

In the preceding pages I have shared with you what I have learned and seen over a period of several years. The fourteen moneymaking ideas that I have presented in detail so far (there will be more at the end of this book) have a common denominator. They can all be started part-time with little or no investment and they can all be successfully run from your home or a friend's home, as long as it contains an appropriate area.

8. NO GAMBLE

You may wonder why I so strongly advocate home business. The reason is very simple. Home business is the most logical approach for a beginner in the business world. Used wisely, it can almost reduce the gamble of going into business for yourself to no gamble at all. The two largest reasons for the failure of a new business is general and flagrant mismanagement, and under-capitalization, with the latter far in the lead. Millions of dollars are lost annually by aspiring entrepreneurs. Some of these failures stole away the life savings of people who had the dream of owning their own business. All too often those people become the prey of the predator in the business world. They are sold costly machinery, equipment, and fixtures, when the same end could have been accomplished at one-tenth of the starting cost. They long-term lease an office or shop facility much larger than needed at the time. All of these things, combined with the costs of telephone, heat, lights, water, various taxes, and all the many other costs of operation, leave them about the same chance as a snowball in a blast furnace.

We go into business primarily for one reason: to build something for ourselves instead of for an employer, thereby enjoying all of the fruits of *our* labor. Thus the only thing that really counts is the bottom line, or how much of our endeavors result in profit in our wallets for us to enjoy.

My wife and I enjoyed a basement-operated business that produced a comfortable income. Time was ours, and we did what we wanted to do, when we wanted to do it. What more could you ask? Several acquaintances of ours, involved in the same line of work, many times chided us about our lack of an office in a professional location. When we compared gross earnings, we started out at about the same level, but by the time we deducted their various overheads, they wound up with only 50% to 60% of the profits which we received. They were always stumped for an answer when I shot this question to them: "Why should we decrease our earnings? Also, you have to keep your office open from eight to five whether you are busy or not. When we are not busy, we simply go upstairs to our home, relax, read, watch TV, work in the garden or yard. If the phone does happen to ring, we can always skip downstairs and answer it." Most of the time my reasoning would go right over their heads. This attitude would make me cry—cry all the way to the bank.

What I am trying to impress on you is *don't play follow the leader*; life is much too short. Be your own person. Be objective, be creative, and it will pay off with handsome dividends. You can own your own business, limit your liability, and enjoy the benefit derived from business ownership, without gambling your last dollar on a single roll of the dice. If you play it smart, you can try a business; if it fails, you simply try another and another, until you have a perfect fit—and there *is* one that will fit you!

Benjamin Franklin once said, "Keep thy shop, and thy shop will keep thee." Franklin was a person of steadfast independence, and had no interest in working for others. To him that was a sign of bondage and slavery. If you have read this far you probably have some misgivings about your own job. You already may be in a position of servitude yourself. The only way to overcome that position is with your own business, so your time and money belong to you alone.

You may feel that most of the businesses I talk about require salesmanship. Many people adamantly declare they could never be a salesperson, nor do they have any desire to try. I felt this way myself originally. We completely overlook the fact that we are born into this life selling. As babies we cried until we convinced our parents of our sincerity in being hungry; and that was just the start. Since that time we have been selling everyone around us on our ability to excel—teachers, friends, co-workers and employers, even husbands, wives, and sweethearts. Think about it. The only real difference between us and a highly paid professional salesperson is that he *does* get paid—we don't.

As a business owner you must ask people to do business with you. The process is very simple. You explain what you are doing and why it would benefit them. You promise them to do everything to the best of your ability, and then you live up to your promise. Now, isn't that simple? Why, it's pretty much what you told your employer in that job interview before you went to work for him, isn't it? It is also precisely what every good salesman, every good business owner, says to his customers. And when you want a raise in pay in your own business, you simply ask a few more people to buy your services or products.

As a home business owner you should develop greater earnings and enjoy many more tax advantages than before. It could change your entire lifestyle, including the home you inhabit, the car you drive, the way you entertain, and the people you know. As you succeed you will attract other successful people into your circle of associations and you will be invited to participate in their circles. You will be exposed to new ideas and educational processes. Take the time to listen to other people. One very wise multimillionaire octogenarian, an active businessperson despite his age, told me that he *listened* to everyone; he had never met a person from whom he could not learn at least something.

As your business changes your lifestyle, so will it change your net financial worth. One of the greatest feelings in life is to quit being someone's employee through building a business of your own. You nurture, shape, and build your business until you prosper and can enjoy some of the life you have always imagined. But then you need to do some serious thinking about where you are headed. I am a firmer believer in diversification; in other words, don't put all your eggs in one basket. You may become content with the niche that you develop through your own business, but most of us soon seek higher goals. We do this through diversified investments. It may be stocks and bonds, investment in other people's business, or even a secondary business of our own; or it could be in real estate, which has been called, "The Basis of All Wealth." It is this last diversified investment that I really want to discuss. I will not pretend to be the all-knowing professional in real estate investment. In this realm, I rely on the experience of others.

Real estate investment has paid huge dividends to scores of people whom I personally know. One fellow was buried in personal bills; creditors were threatening repossession and legal actions of all types. He went to them and somehow managed to stall them. He then opened a small business (no investment) of his own. As he started making money, he diverted 25% of his net income into real estate investment. Today he is well on the road to attaining his millionaire designation. I know another couple who diverted some of their business profits into real estate. In less than two years their additional monthly earnings are close to the $2,000.00 mark. The list of such stories is endless. If you ever consider real estate, I strongly recommend reading *How to Wake Up the Financial Genius Inside of You* by Mark Oliver Haroldson.

9. *HOME BUSINESS II*

Following are more moneymaking prospects based on Mental Maneuverability and Manipulation. These home businesses are presented as examples of unique ways to get more for your money with less effort, and pathways to continue to capitalize on your new knowledge and power.

$ECRETARIAL $ERVICE

If you are a good typist with an adequate command of the English language, and own a typewriter or can rent one, how about starting a secretarial service based in your home? Many small businesses have correspondence to be done, yet cannot employ a full-time secretary. You might even include a resume-typing service for people looking for work. I was introduced to a woman who admitted to making over $1,000.00 per month from the forty or fifty small business clients she had. She simply contacted small businesses and told them of her service; before long she had all the work she wanted.

MAILING FOR MONEY

A good couple business is sending out special occasion cards, such as on birthdays, anniversaries, and holidays. Many businesses, large and small, have clients they keep on a perpetual mailing list for continuing public relations. You should first find someone who will wholesale you the greeting cards. To expand your profit potential, you then contact other businesses—real estate and insurance offices are prime targets. Offer them a package deal. You supply the card and stamp, and address and mail it as well. For this you charge a flat fee. Some prices I have heard are as high as $1.50 to $2.00 per individual mailing.

COLLECTING CHECKS (AND MONEY TOO!)

Have rubber stamps made saying, "$10.00 service charge to be assessed on this check if returned by bank. Charge will be paid by ____________________." Obviously, the blank space will be signed by the writer of the check. You then take this stamp to places of business, and make this offer to supply them with a stamp like this free, if they will let you collect the checks. If you are successful in your collection efforts, they will receive the full face amount of the check and you will keep the $10.00 service charge. This is a good deal for them and for you.

DANCING TO THE BANK

A dance studio in your home is an excellent business for husband-and-wife teams if you are good dancers. With no expensive overhead, you could probably run your business cut-rate, have plenty of students, and reap a nice extra income. Advertise through the personal or instruction column in newspapers; handbills also may work well. After attaining some experience, you might recruit other part-time instructors to teach things in which you are not proficient. You could offer ballroom, modern, ballet—a whole curriculum of dancing.

SHORT HAULS FOR LONG GAINS

Have a pickup truck or access to one? Light hauling jobs are in demand. You might contact small furniture, appliance stores, etc., for their excess hauling jobs, or for contract hauling when their trucks may be out of service. Also, you might find jobs hauling for individuals—young marrieds, senior citizens—practically everyone has a need from time to time. Simple classified advertising, word-of-mouth, or cards posted in grocery stores and laundromats should net you quite a bit of business.

CALLING ALL COURIERS

Many businesses such as law firms, real estate offices, and banks need a local courier service for pickup and delivery of important papers. Often businesses and offices want to transmit documents, papers, and bills without waiting for postal service which can take two or three days at times, even within the same town. You could charge a fee of 20 25¢ per mile, plus a flat fee of $10.00 to $15.00 and up, depending on the importance of the papers and speed of delivery necessary.

NOT FOR THE BIRDS

The bird business has been conducted from the bedroom of an apartment in New York City. Birds are ideal pets for other apartment dwellers. They require little room, do not have to be taken for walks, and are reasonably quiet. When they do make noise, neighbors don't seem to object as much as they might to other pets. One couple sold birds from their apartment; dealing canaries, finches, parakeets, cockatoos and cockatiels, and even some parrots. They also sold feed, cages, accessories, and bird books. They arranged with their customers to buy back unhatched eggs, which they incubated. If you are a bird lover and know something about them, this could be an ideal occupation.

TEACHING AT HOME

If you're proficient in carpentry, electrical, plumbing, heating, or mechanical work, there are always people interested in such skills, who would pay a price to learn. You could set up the trade school in your garage or basement, two or three evenings a week. I knew a fellow doing this. He not only taught classes, but offered a future consulting benefit where, if involved in a project, you could call him for additional information. On occasion, he would even drive over to help with the problem. He charged just like a doctor making house calls, and is doing well with his home business.

One successful lady I know works out of her basement teaching sewing and knitting. She has about a dozen sewing machines and three or four knitting machines. She offers a three-week class to get you started; after that you are on your own, but you can continue to work in her basement, on her machines, for an hourly rental fee until you can afford to buy your own machine, which she can sell you. She also carries a selection of fabrics, threads and yarns, plus many patterns. She even has outlets lined up where she can sell items that her students manufacture.

STREET CORNER FLOWER STAND

This one is a real sleeper. Don't let the size of this enterprise fool you. You can buy flowers in quantity from a floral shop, wholesale, and then sell them from a street corner with a simple hand-lettered sign. Your profits are limited only by the amount of time you want to put in, and by the traffic on the corner you select (check city ordinances and licenses required). A friend of mine told me that he knew of one such street corner proprietor who was earning on the average of $150.00 a day.

WORKING VACATIONS

House, plant and pet care for vacationers is a service my family has used several times, and can be run from your own home. A number of people would rather not take their pets to boarding kennels while they are gone, so you could perform several services for them while they are away from home. The business we knew was a family operation. They would keep a key to your home; when you were gone they would come in and feed your pets and let them out to run in the yard, pick up the mail from the mailbox, gather the newspapers, water the plants, check your house; they even had ways of being notified in case of fire or burglary. At times they were handling twenty-five or thirty houses daily with a minimum rate of $6.00 each house per day—some fees were higher depending on services performed.

RISE AND SHINE

Running your own wake-up and conversation service is a great possibility for people desiring to earn money from the use of their home phone. Quite a few people do not wake up from an alarm clock, and would subscribe to this service. Because of different wake-up time requirements, you could handle forty or fifty clients over a two-hour period of time in the morning, and charge $10.00 per month for each. Also, busy families with an aged parent living alone would pay you to telephone and check that senior three or four times a day; another $10.00 or $15.00 per client per month possible, (the rate for this is somewhat lower than wake-up service). Classified advertising in the newspaper, referral, and cards on community bulletin boards should do.

CRAFTS ON CONSIGNMENT

People young and old make gift items at home of unique beauty and value. Line up twenty-five or thirty of these people who make home crafts. You then take pictures of the items with a Polaroid camera, and this collection becomes your catalogue. Next show your catalogue to gift shops and retail stores; they may buy outright—you take a middleman fee. If not—you can display the items on consignment and take a commission when they sell. Craft and hobby shops can supply you with names of people making these crafts, or you can just leave your telephone number with them and they could have their customers contact you.

FLEA MARKET MAGNATE

I met a man and his wife who did well in the flea market circuit. Through the week they traveled around various neighborhoods, offering for free to pick up old toys, clothes, furniture, appliances, and anything else they could find, and haul them away. They then would sort through the load, fix what they could, and haul the rest to the dump. On weekends they took the salable items to a flea market, rented a booth, and made up to five or six hundred dollars for their efforts.

THINK SHARP

Lawn mower and saw sharpening service is always in demand everywhere, and can be learned easily. The equipment may cost you a little bit to start, but if you use some of my formulas for saving money, it shouldn't take long to acquire the necessary funds. I have seen advertisements for training and equipment in the magazine, *Income Opportunities*, probably available at your local magazine stand. In fact, the fellow I took my sharpening work to started this way and was doing a landslide business.

MONKEY BUSINESS

How about a "Rent a Clown or Gorilla" sideline? Dressed up in either one of those suits, you're guaranteed to liven up any party. Even if you're one of the inhibited souls, you may lose the inhibitions since you won't be recognized (you may also find it a lot of fun). I spoke with a one-time college student who had a costume place make him both outfits. He then contacted business places to hire him as a public relations gimmick. He then cavorted around to attract customers, even signed autographs for children. He now has expanded and rents himself to parties and other social, business, and political functions. He must do well, judging by his car and home. He eventually gave up a profession to do this full-time.

ROUTE TO SUCCESS

A laundry and dry cleaning route is almost something of the past, and maybe that is precisely why it can be a real winner, particularly if you already own a van-type vehicle. You could start out right in your own neighborhood or apartment house just part-time. I suggest you contact your favorite dry cleaning and laundry establishment and see what you can work out. The one I investigated was set up as follows: the dry cleaner and laundry raised his counter price by about 15%, and then paid the contract routeman a total of 30% commission on the gross charges. The routeman I interviewed worked in a bank, and therefore had almost three hours a day to work his little part-time business (also Saturdays). Believe it or not, he was picking up and delivering an average of $80.00 worth of cleaning and laundry a day, $24.00 for him times five days equals $120.00; Saturdays he picked up and delivered $300.00 worth (his piece of the action—$90.00), for a grand total of $210.00 per week. Not too bad, eh? Why would anyone pay 15% premium for pick-up and delivery? To save gas, of course. Why would the dry cleaner pay 15% commission? Obviously, more business volume without advertising.

CORNER THE MARKET

Street corner selling seems to be in vogue. I have seen this activity in many towns. I quizzed several of these card table vendors, and walked away amazed. One young lady really impressed me, and volunteered a lot of information when she learned that I was questioning her for details to put in a book. In fact, she went so far as to prove her point with purchase invoices from her supplier, which I later verified.

This woman was purchasing on the average of $93.00 worth of merchandise a day. What did she sell? All kinds of novelties, specializing in dolls, stuffed animals, and toys. Her profit ranged from 35% to 75% on each item, with an average of about 48%, or $44.64 a day, which adds up to $223.20 a week or thereabouts. She worked only five days a week, no Saturdays. She said it wasn't profitable to compete with the stores on Saturdays. Incidentally, on the weekdays she worked twelve noon to six o'clock, covering lunch times and after-work traffic. Why do people buy from a street corner stand? I don't really know—curiosity, I suppose, and then impulse takes over.

CURBS OF SILVER

If you want something light, easy, and quick, curb painting might fit the bill. A retired gentleman on social security does well with this project. It would even be great for younger people, men or women, or kids. He went to a local art store, bought four-inch high number stencils for less than five dollars, purchased some cans of spray paint in black and silver, and went into business for less than $15.00. He paints street numbers on curbs. You have seen them, I'm sure. First he goes up and down a street contacting property owners interested in having their house number painted on the curb. He only charges $1.00 per numbering, and gets a lot of orders. When he has accumulated about twenty-five orders, he begins painting, and wraps the whole deal up in one afternoon from start to finish. If you take a look at a numbered curb, I think you will readily see how it's done. First, spray on approximately a six-inch by ten-inch background in silver paint, then using your number stencils, spray the house's address in black on top of the silver field. In a short period of time, and with some practicing at home, almost anyone can master this particular business.

NO START-UP MONEY REQUIRED

If you are financially embarrassed to the point where you cannot even afford to invest anything in your own business, but still want to try, and feel you have the ability to become a direct salesperson on a commercial level dealing with other business people, you might consider selling advertising specialities: imprinted matches, ballpoint pens, key chains, and the 1001 items given away by businesses for advertising purposes. The advertising specialities company that I purchase from was started for the price of a postage stamp a very few years ago. It now has nice offices, warehouse space, and about twenty employees. The owner drives a Cadillac Eldorado Barritz, belongs to an exclusive country club, lives in a custom-built home. He was a high school dropout and then a general laborer prior to his present success. The owner of this company tells me that this opportunity still exists for the real hustler. There are several manufacturers that will help you to get into this business with no cost. You will find them advertising for agents in such excellent magazines as *Speciality Salesman, Money-Making Opportunities*, and others of this type. (I have listed two more in the last section of this book.)

TELEPHONE TRADER

An accident victim confined to a wheelchair has built a thriving business in exchanging and trading durable goods. He primarily handles automobiles, furniture, appliances, and tools, but will list almost anything, and he conducts his entire business by telephone and mail.

Here's how it works: you have an item that you no longer need or want. You would call this trade expert and tell him what you would take in trade for your item. He generally asks you for at least five acceptable alternates. He then makes a card file for the one-time registration fee of $5.00 plus 5% of the value of your item when it is successfully traded. He tells me that charging $5.00 for registration keeps the curiosity seekers and small, valueless items away and allows him to work with serious traders.

If you are beginning to think this is a peanuts business, think again. He recently concluded a three-way trade involving almost $120,000.00 in total values. Keep in mind he charges each party 5% of the traded item value, so in reality he is actually collecting 10% of the gross value of trade. On the three-way trade he made $12,000.00. Of course, he doesn't pull this coup every day, but then he doesn't need to. This enterprising businessman anticipates earning in excess of $40,000.00 per year, and currently has over three thousand registrations on file. In fact, he is now considering the purchase of a desk-top computer. He says his loss by people refusing to pay him is less than 3%; however, on larger deals he does have a legal document drawn by an attorney that he requires his customers to sign. His only expense in starting this business was about $80.00 worth of classified advertising in the local newspaper for one month, from then on he has operated by word of mouth. After all, almost everyone has something he would like to trade for a new and different item.

I have been telling you about cases that all seem to have the same common factors: (1) need and desire; (2) positive attitude and implementation; then (3) profitability and success; and all are equal ingredients in **M**ental **M**aneuverability and **M**anipulation—**MMM.** The factor I would like to explore with you is the first—need and desire.

In many cases it appears that something of a traumatic nature triggers thought processes and motivates one to success. You must know several people who have suffered major setbacks or catastrophic events, and then went on to achieve great successes. Perhaps severe hardship is a necessary element of **MMM**. However, whether you are experiencing an actual hardship condition (by your measure) or not, and unless you have everything you desire and the freedom of your time to do as you choose, you are a member of the vast majority that is in serious financial trouble. Most people delude themselves by feeling secure in the fact that they have the ability to meet the monthly house mortgage and car payments, put food on the table, and sock away a couple of bucks for a rainy day. Well, this is all right if it is what you want and that ability would continue, but in most cases it won't.

The life insurance industry made an in-depth study of this syndrome and has come up with some very alarming statistics that are all too true. Out of every ten working people who reach the age of sixty-five, two will be dead, four will be dependent on family or others for their support, three will be just scraping by, and one will be totally self-sufficient. If you want something to shake you even further, sometime visit a state, county, or community-supported home for the aged and witness the loss of identity some of these people suffer and the pure despondency they represent. I am not being critical of these institutions, because in most cases they are doing the best they can on limited allocated funds.

Now I am going to offer an example, the exact opposite of the above picture for your consideration. I know a couple in their late seventies. Believe it or not, he still participates in some leisurely downhill skiing, and can well afford it. They own a beautiful winter home in a warm, moderate climate and a summer A-frame chateau in a picturesque mountain setting. They trade their Lincoln Continental every couple of years because of high mileage from extensive travel. They also try to take a major trip once a year. This year they are going to spend a month in Spain. They enjoy holiday seasons with grandchildren and great-grandchildren, as the kids are always willing to visit with this perennially young-in-mind couple. The astounding part of this story is that these people have been living like this for over twenty years, ever since they sold their business and retired; a business, which I might add, that was started on a shoestring.

What is my point? Simply this: which would you rather be—old, forgotten, barely existing under someone else's control; or forever young-in-mind and spirit, loved and genuinely independent at any age? The choice is yours to make, but each day that goes by gives you one less day in which to control your own destiny.

Take inventory of your present situation, honestly appraise where you are headed. If you have the slightest doubt or misgiving about your future, then you and your family are facing traumatic and catastrophic upheaval at some point in your lives. If success does sometimes spring from life's ashes and tragedy, you may consider yourself already qualified by that rule, and completely entitled to all the happiness that success will bring. All you have to do is gain knowledge, then implement your plan for personal profitability.

10. PURCHASE POWER

In order to round out the general education that this book is meant to provide, I outline five more sound, profitable businesses, plus additional ways to live better by maximizing your purchasing powers in several areas.

STARTING WITH ART

A few months ago I was contacted by an art representative. Let's call her Jennie. I became totally enthralled and captivated by this vivacious person's positive attitude toward life, people, and her business. She had suffered a bad marriage and, subsequently, a divorce. She had two children to raise, a drawer full of bills and no money or income. Jennie started work as a waitress, and in that very job found her opportunity.

You see, one of her regular coffee customers was a young art student who showed a great natural talent. His painting ability had already progressed beyond his art education. One day he brought several paintings into the restaurant to show Jennie, and they were decidedly very good. He admitted that he had not done well in trying to sell any of his artwork. He also admitted that he was shy and not good at approaching people to buy his pictures. Jennie felt a little sorry for this artist and decided to help.

She already had an idea. The pictures in the restaurant where she worked were old, faded, and just copies anyway, a detraction from the decor. Jennie removed the old pictures from the walls and hung the young artist's paintings in their place. Later that day the restaurant owner returned and initially was upset until Jennie told him they were on loan for a week. A business was born that day.

A week later, as Jennie started to take the paintings down and replace them with the old ones, the owner of the restaurant asked if he might buy them. A deal was negotiated between him and the artist, and the paintings were purchased.

Jennie became an art representative, and now at times represents more than one thousand artists all over the country. She has several salespeople working for her in the same fashion. They customarily work with commercial and business people, but in some cases with individuals through interior decorators. Jennie and each one of her salespeople carry a portfolio of 8" x 10" photographs of some of the paintings they have in stock. They will interview a prospect, find out what subject he or she is interested in, such as animals, flowers, landscapes and so on, and also what colors the person likes. Jennie then offers to hang the selected paintings in the customer's place of business or home for a period of one week, or even up to one month, free, with no obligation to purchase. Jennie told me that under this plan most people wind up buying at least one painting, and often several.

Why do they buy? Jennie's prices for original art are usually much lower than a gallery's, even including her 25% commission. Jennie has cut out several middlemen profits plus offers a very personalized service which people appreciate.

Jennie tells me that she personally has sold as much as $20,000.00 worth of art in a single week. At 25% her commission for a week's work was $5,000.00; not bad for an ex-waitress. Jennie has yet to invest a single dime in her business, and continues to operate in the same manner as when she started, except on a much larger scale. She contacts talented artists and offers to sell their work for them. They keep her supplied with paintings on a consignment basis, even paying the cost of shipping the paintings to her. Jennie says that now 70% of her sales is referral and repeat business.

STEAMING AHEAD

This nice little business is netting the owner about $400.00 a week while he pursues a career as an aeronautical engineer. His total investment to get started was $1,000.00 for an eight-year-old Chevy pickup and $350.00 for a used commercial-grade steam cleaner to mount in the bed of the pickup. He then contacted grocery stores, restaurants, pastry shops, and other businesses that would require steam cleaning services of their food racks and tables for sanitation purposes to meet regulations. His gross business income now is about $3,000.00 per month. He has hired two efficient young women to run it for him. One he pays $600.00 a month, the other $500.00 a month. It costs him about $200.00 a month for gas, insurance, and upkeep on his equipment, leaving him about $1,700.00 a month for his net profit. Incidentally, the place of business supplies the water needs for his steam cleaner. His largest accounts are grocery stores on a contract basis. He not only steams their freezer and produce racks, but their grocery carts as well, and does minor repair such as replacing damaged wheels, axles, cart straightening, etc. He averages about $200.00 per month per store and has ten under contract. His heaviest physical labor in this neat little business is counting his money.

SAND CANDLE SECRETS

This and the next two examples are started separately, and all made money. Then the people involved got together, combined their talents, and now look like they are well on their way to becoming big business. The first husband-and-wife team made gift items in their garage, such as decoupaged wall plaques, dry floral arrangements, and then their big speciality—sand candles. I had seen sand candles in gift shops and had always supposed those beautiful creations would take a block-long industrial complex for their manufacturing. Not true. With about fifty bucks, a little practice and patience, almost anyone can duplicate those gorgeous gift candles.

Rather than try to tell you how to make them, I will tell you how to get complete information free and quick—from your public library. I began to research the subject of sand candles in the obvious way, through craft shops. They weren't much help at all. My research was not turning out as complete as I hoped, so I went to some manufacturers to learn some of the secrets of sand candle manufacturing. Boy, were they a closed-mouth group! So, in desperation as I have so many times in the past, I stopped in at our local public library and asked the librarian to help. She, as always, was very accommodating and soon located professional books on sand candle casting, proper temperatures, types of wax, equipment, the works.

Anyway, the couple involved in this business had been selling their wares to family, friends, work associates, and some gift stores for a while, quite successfully, when they decided to expand their business. And this brings us to the next idea.

RAISING FUNDS, RAISING PROFITS

Fund raising can be exciting, rewarding, and fun, provided you have the right products at the right prices—which is where a small fund raiser may have a few problems.

Let me take a moment to explain what fund raising is. It is basically the business of raising money for schools, churches, charities, youth groups, service clubs, and a whole array of other projects. This multimillion-dollar-a-year business involves both large and small companies. I am sure you have been exposed to it; kids selling candy and a host of other items, adults selling brooms, cake, light bulbs, you name it; all in the name of their favorite charity or project.

Now, this couple I am going to tell you about had been in fund raising sales for a couple of years with some small degree of success. The way their business generally worked was they would buy some item from a manufacturer at about 50% of retail value, then tack on 12% to 15% for their trouble, and then let people trying to raise money sell it. This last group would make from 35% to 38% for their particular club or charity. This worked well enough, but there were some limits to what our couple could buy for this purpose. They were continually on the lookout for gift items that were new, exciting, and different.

Then providence stepped in. Quite by accident, they first became social acquaintances of the people in the previous story.

The day came when these four people put their heads together, decided to combine their talents, and see if they could help each other. Their new endeavor was a smashing success; their business doubled and redoubled almost overnight, it seemed. The giftmakers had to greatly expand their manufacturing facilities, and the fund raisers accepted more and more groups to supply. People become tired of buying the same old things from fund raising projects. When these new creative gift items were presented by their favoirte charitable organization, they bought and bought and bought. It would seem that the end of a rainbow and its pot of gold had been reached, but not quite yet—read on to the next subject.

THE PARTY APPROACH

Party plan sales have made a number of people anywhere from a small part-time income to whopping big-figure earnings for many years, all without forbidding investments on the part of the small entrepreneurs. There are many fine companies sponsoring this type of business. Some of the largest outfits are Tupperware, Sarah Coventry, Rubber Maid, and Mary Kay. Their training methods practically guarantee that you will earn money. The amount is up to you and your individual application. If you would enjoy meeting people in a hostess's home, in a combined business and social atmosphere, I would strongly recommend that you examine this type of business. I think you might be happily surprised at the possibilities.

One such couple I know have been involved in party plan sales for several years, and were loyal to the company that gave them their start. However, for the last couple of years they had felt the itch to proceed on to bigger things, such as their own company in the party plan business. However, they were unable to find the products they need to start their business, until one day when their oldest son brought home a sample of a beautiful plaque he and his classmates would soon be selling to raise money for their senior class trip. The plaque had been manufactured by the couple who also made sand candles, and distributed to the school by the fund raising couple. This last couple, the party planners, soon got in touch with the gift manufacturing couple and shortly thereafter held the first of what has become many meetings together. The party planners had found just what they were looking for: products with quality and customer appeal. It took very little time for them to open their own home party plan specializing in home decor and decorating items. They started out doing very well, and continue to increase sales as each month goes by.

Each couple in this triple twosome acts independently in the respective businesses, but the businesses complement each other and the owners have become good friends. Each couple is interested in the other's total success and is willing to help in any way it can. I think the last three stories capture perfectly the spirit and power of **MMM**. Each of these couples were doing all right, but far from great. The people involved, however, did have the ability to seize upon an opportunity, tailor it to their needs and ideals, then guide it toward a destination providing security and happiness for all those involved. Perhaps you, too, have friends or relatives who could provide talent or energy toward a common goal. If so, don't be greedy to the point of not sharing your ideas with someone who could help you both achieve the status of *Armchair Millionaire* through **MMM**.

Anything I have to offer beyond the last three examples would seem almost anticlimactic, but I have saved this next one because it contains a little of everything I have tried to impress upon you—trauma, need and desire, positive attitude and implementation, and finally, profitability and success. But this tale also includes one other tremendously important word, which used wrongly will result in disaster, and used rightly will lay the world and its treasures at your feet—*ego*.

FRANKS WITH DISTINCTION

The person this success story concerns is someone I met about six months ago while doing some business research. As I came to know this person better, his personal courage, sense of humor, adaptability, and compassion for other people began to emerge as a model that I think **MMM** can help most. This person talked to me only after I assured him that his name would not be made public, so I, therefore, will simply refer to him as my "friend."

My friend was a career police officer who had worked hard to become a respected citizen of his community, and a competent detective on his way up. Although born of poor parents in an area one level above welfare acres, he managed to scrape and fight his way to a decent education and career position. Then one day position, career, and future came to an abrupt end through a job-related serious injury. Upon his recovery, which left him with a minor disability, he was medically retired from the police force. My friend was aware of the mandatory medical retirement provisions for serious injury resulting in any degree of disability, so while convalescing he entered a technical trades institute and received an associate degree in electronic technology.

After entering the work force market, he discovered employers did not want to hire him for a couple of reasons. One, he was an older graduate than they were looking for. My friend was in his middle thirties. And two, he had his medical retirement income. It's surprising, but many companies feel that having a steady outside income might weaken a person's dependence on their paycheck and, therefore, create an overly independent employee.

Now we come to the interesting part of this saga. My friend disposed of his home, packed up his family, and moved out West to see if he could find a new future, only to run into the same hiring restrictions. Finally, he gave up job hunting and decided that the only route would be a business of his own. But what?

By this time his funds were too limited to purchase any type of going business that would provide an adequate income. Then an idea dawned on him. Something quite common where he came from in the East was missing in his new adopted town, a little insignificant business that apparently no one had ever bothered to start. The business was a roll-around street vendor hot dog cart complete with umbrella, featuring Coney Island hot dogs, popcorn, and soft drinks.

After locating one of the little carts through a restaurant supplier in a nearby larger city, my friend was ready to set up his business. Local licensing was reasonably easy to take care of. The humorous part of this story is my friend's approach to merchandising his frankfurter cart and himself. Imagine this if you can: he dressed up in a tasteful three-piece suit, white shirt and tie, then stood on a busy downtown street corner serving franks, popcorn, and soft drinks. This distinctive showmanship had the desired effect, exactly as my friend had planned. Well-dressed executives and secretaries from fancy office buildings nearby patronized the well-dressed street corner vendor every day. And while they quietly laughed among themselves, my friend was building what has become an extremely profitable business. Today he operates in excess of a dozen of these hot dog carts manned by venders he hires. He also has office and warehouse space, several other employees including salespeople, and most recently a multistate distributorship in a very fast-moving speciality food product. All of this was accomplished on a hundred-dollar original investment and about a month's work.

The reason I saved the next story until last and particularly wanted to share it with you, was to point out a failing in psychological attitude that many of us, including myself, are or have been guilty of: sometimes ego does not allow us to be the success we could be.

TOO GOOD FOR SUCCESS?

I know an accountant (C.P.A. level) with a large firm. His annual income is around $27,00.00 per year, but he readily admits he hates his job and really doesn't enjoy his profession. His younger brother was a maverick-type person who barely made it through high school, bummed around for a few years, and eventually started an auto junkyard business with borrowed money. When the younger brother started to gain success and acquire prominence, he offered several times to include his older brother in the growing business with no investment. He needed trustworthy help and wanted to share his prosperity with his older brother.

This very generous offer was turned down as many times as it was offered, even though the older brother made the statement on a couple of occasions that he thought the junkyard business might be fun, and surely not as pressure-ridden as his job.

Why, then, the refusal? *Ego.* The older brother explained that he would be lowering his standards in the eyes of friends and business associates, wasting a professional education, and his in-laws would be absolutely mortified. They were very proud that their daughter had the good sense to marry a professional man!

Today the younger brother, his wife and children are a respected and popular family within their city. In fact, he was just voted into an important city office. They share and enjoy life. I might mention that the younger brother's annual income exceeds the $150,000.00 mark. The older brother labors on in his accounting job, steadily growing more unhappy and bitter. His health is deteriorating because of the mental pressures; even his family life is rocky and troubled, all because of a misguided ego.

The point is this: it really doesn't matter whether you are a doctor or a street corner vender, as long as you are happy with what you are doing. When you are happy is when you will do your best; that, coupled with knowledge, will bring you respect, success, and prosperity—I guarantee it.

11. MORE PROSPERITY

In this chapter I will discuss many different ideas, but all with a common goal. When you start making a nice income there will be a time when you may begin to act like a kid with a ten-dollar bill in the proverbial candy store. If you do, it will simply prove that you are human. Go ahead, have your fling. In time it will pass.

We have explored numerous ways and methods where other people have used **MMM** to become highly successful. Now, to fulfill my obligation to you and to round out the education that you have paid for with the purchase of this book, I caution you to watch out for the multitudes of people out there just waiting to get a part of what you have earned. They even might take it all, if you let them. If you can learn to earn money with your newly found **MMM** knowledge, you can just as easily learn how to *get a dollar's value for every dollar you spend,* another highly important facet of **MMM**.

It is not my intent to inspire general paranoia, but first of all I want to stress the importance of carefully selecting the people from whom you require services—doctors, dentists, lawyers, accountants, real estate and insurance agents, auto mechanics, appliance service people, carpenters, electricians, and so on. Many people will expend more time and effort on the purchase of a ten-dollar article of clothing than they would on the selection of a person they may pay hundreds or thousands of dollars for services. I have seen people put their money, futures, and even their lives in the hands of someone they knew nothing about, simply by picking a name out of the yellow pages at random.

Here is a sure-fire formula for the selection of professional, technical, or trade people that is 98% guaranteed, and will work anyplace at any time. I refer to it simply as the **Five-Deep Selection Process.** The original concept was supplied to me by a highly successful business person. I had noticed that whenever this person required help or professional guidance of any kind he always managed to obtain the best possible service; even the boy who mowed his lawn was the best in town.

Now for the **Five-Deep Selection Process.** Let's use a family doctor as an example. For some reason you do not have one, or are unhappy with the one you do have, and want to make a change. This is what you do: ask a friend, relative or co-worker if he can recommend a good doctor that he has used or has personal knowledge of. If he does recommend someone, ask him how he became acquainted with the doctor. If he says by accident or yellow pages or noticed the office while driving by, then forget this doctor for right now. But if he says the doctor was recommended by someone else, then find out who that someone else is, since you'll need to contact him. If you feel self-conscious about asking for this person's phone number, look it up in the telephone directory or call information. Tell the second party that you were told by the previous party (identify) that the doctor in question is an excellent physician, and you wondered how he felt about the doctor. If he says the same thing, then ask him how he became acquainted with the doctor. If the contact was through another party, get the name and, once again, follow the same procedure. Do this until you have five personal referrals recommending the doctor. When you complete this, you can rest pretty well assured that you have located a top-notch physician.

Apply this procedure not only to doctors, but to lawyers, accountants, service repair shops, etcetera. Find the right person to do a professional job, and don't be taken in by some individual's slick sales pitch about how good he is or how much he wants to serve you or how cheaply he will work. It may cost you dearly in the long run. Unfortunately, the attachment of a professional or technical designation after a person's name does not necessarily make him someone in whom to entrust confidence.

The old adage, "An ounce of prevention is worth a pound of cure," is one of the most profound statements I know. So start now to build your list of credible, ethical, and honest people from whom you may require some type of service. Do it before you ever need it. If the occasion does arise, all you have to do is pick up the phone for professional assistance by someone you can *trust*.

CHANGING LIFESTYLES WITH "MMM"

Now, as a final success story, I would like to tell you about a family my wife and I became acquainted with a couple of years ago. I consider what they have accomplished one of the finest examples of **MMM** that I know of. They have traded a worrisome, pressure-ridden lifestye for one of prosperous serenity, complete with a secure financial foundation that will last the rest of their lives.

After sixteen or seventeen years, this couple—Paul and Ann—had become the perfect mirrored reflection of the corporate lifestyle; a position in the higher echelon and hierarchy of the company was easily within reach. They owned a large comfortable home in suburbia, prestige automobiles, a country club membership, and many of the other amenities of life. Everything should have been perfect . . . only it wasn't. For within their hearts was a constant yearning and desire, growing stronger as the days passed, and a certain knowledge that even though life was being very good to them, there were elements missing, subtracting from their total happiness. (How many of us are now experiencing, or have experienced this paradox?)

Three years ago, after some intensive soul-searching, Paul and Ann reached a decision on what they really wanted from life for themselves and their sons, and it wasn't the corporate and suburban lifestyle they were presently involved in.

Paul and Ann both had at times experienced semi-rural environments when they were growing up, and believed this would be an excellent atmosphere for their family and new lifestyle. The whole family had a fondness for animals and nature, also for a slower paced routine that only rural living can provide. But, how do you go about changing from a $60,000.00-a-year corporation executive to a farmer without risking your entire financial future in the process? For less innovative and creative people this may well have been an insurmountable problem. Not for Paul and Ann, though. They looked the problem straight in the eye, accepted it, and then turned it around to become a positive influence.

Paul and Ann had determined that their total net worth was in the vicinity of $60,000.00 to $80,000.00.

This would include liquidation of their home, in which they had a nice equity, the sale of a rental property, plus about $10,000.00 cash on hand. They decided to use a $60,000.00 estimate for their lifestyle change, and it is well they did, because their properties did not bring as much as they had hoped. After everything was finalized, they wound up with about $65,000.00 total cash.

Right here is where many people make a disastrous mistake in trying to move to the country. A lot of people are not willing to sacrifice, even on a temporary basis, any of the creature comforts they enjoyed in city living. They seem to expect the best of both worlds, often times overburdening themselves financially to the point of guaranteed failure. You would be surprised at the number of people moving to the country who expect to purchase a house at least comparable, and, in a number of cases, better than what they had in the city. In fact, this becomes so important to them that they will settle for less acreage in order to accomplish this end, with a final result of a big home, a large mortgage, high payments, and two or three acres. Property of this size is very hard to do anything with other than create an unusually large yard, which may take all your leisure time just to maintain.

After lengthy discussions and a solid decision as to what they really wanted, Paul and Ann purchased an eighty-acre parcel of ground that fit their budget perfectly. It included a good deep well with crystal clear water, electricity and telephone lines already installed, and even had a pole corral and old house. Although not suitable for remodeling as a residence, the house was excellent for a garage or storage building. In deciding on this property, Paul and Ann passed up the small, picturesque acreages with high prices, located on the outskirts of large metropolitan areas. Instead they chose highly functional property, perfect for light farming or limited ranching, and within a reasonable commuting distance of a medium-sized modern city. The property's cost was about the same as those overpriced small acreage development properties you often see advertised as ranchettes.

Phase one of their plan was now complete with the acquisition of their land, and it was time for the second phase: acquiring a home adequate for their family needs but at a reasonable price that would fit within the remainder of their budgeted money. Their final selection of residence was an exceptionally well built, used fourteen-by-eighty-foot mobile home. It has three bedrooms, two baths, a large living room, and good sized kitchen. All together the mobile home encompassed about 1,100 square feet of living space; much smaller than their previous home, but large and comfortable enough for their future plans.

Paul, Ann and family moved into their new situation more than two years ago. Let me recap their costs at that time, and then discuss their accomplishments, current lifestyle, and final goals. The cost of their eighty acres was $37,000.00, and the cost of the mobile home $11,000.00, for a grand total of $48,000.00. The balance of their $65,000.00 went into improvements, livestock, and equipment, all paid for in cash with no debts owing.

I would like to interject at this point that they bought everything at bargain prices for two reasons: (1) they paid in cash which put them in a very favorable position from the standpoint of negotiation; and (2) they could offer immediate money for what they purchased. (You would be surprised how sellers will discount if you can offer immediate money.)

I made an analysis of what immediate cash purchasing power had actually done for Paul and Ann. Looking at everything they had purchased and comparing with equal offerings, *they had saved themselves 25,000 to 30,000 bucks.* Now, let's take this hypothesis one step further. We will be conservative and estimate the value of their land and home purchase at $80,000.00. Having been in the banking business, it has been my experience that people on the average will pay up to 20% to 25% down on their purchases, and then finance the balance. Using this formula and taking the high side (25% down), would have resulted in a down payment in cash of $20,000.00, leaving a financed balance of $60,000.00. Once again, let's be conservative and say they could have borrowed the $60,000.00 at 10% interest for a period of twenty-five years. They then would have been obligated to pay back the staggering sum of $163,620.00! I shall elaborate on this further at the end of this chapter.

Through the use of good architectural and engineering suggestions, the evolution of Paul and Ann's original fourteen-by-eighty-foot mobile home is nothing short of miraculous, yet something that almost anyone could duplicate with a common sense approach, some advice-seeking, and a willingness to do some physical labor. That mobile home has grown rapidly into a luxury 3,000-square-foot family home—I defy you to identify it as ever having started out as a mobile home.

The beauties of their accomplishments are twofold: firstly, they had a comfortable place to live right where their building project was taking place; and secondly, by not having any particular rush time-frame in which to complete their building project, they were able to take advantage of bargain buys on all the materials they needed.

Now, as to the economics of their project, let me give you a comparison based on prices in our area. Paul and Ann's cost for their 3,000-square-foot former mobile home, including foundation, materials, and even a small amount of hired help, was in the range of $8.00 or $9.00 per square foot. If we take the high figure of $9.00 per square foot, then their 3,000-square-foot luxury home cost approximately $27,000.00. In my area, the lowest new home construction cost I could find was quoted at about $38.00 per square foot, not including the lot. Now, multiply that times Paul and Ann's 3,000 square feet, and we get the depressing sum total of $114,000.00!

Let's try going one step further and say that Paul and Ann would have used their $27,000.00 total as a down payment to finance the construction of a new 3,000-square-foot home, leaving them with an $87,000.00 balance to finance for twenty-five years at 10%. Take a look at their hypothetical loan pay-back figure, friends: $237,249.00. It is any wonder that few of us ever accumulate any significant amount of money in our lives, with all the ways available to give our money to someone else?

I want to share one more of Paul and Ann's secrets with you in regard to transportation. They switched their Z-28 Camaro and Cadillac for older used Jeep Wagoneer station wagons, and this is the explanation that Paul gave me: "Jeep Wagoneers are tough and serviceable. Four-wheel drive vehicles are perfectly adapted to ranch or farm use in good or bad weather, for work or pleasure. And here's one other important fact, the body style—except grill—is exactly the same from 1965 to 1980; even newer grills can be interchanged for old ones with very slight modifications." One of Paul's Jeep Wagoneer wagons, that I had thought to be new, was in reality a 1966 model that he had face-lifted, with a current model grill, including square headlights, interior out of another late model Wagoneer that had been wrecked, new paint, and some minor chrome work.

If you were to see this vehicle on the street, you would bet money that it is a new $12,000.00 unit instead of a fourteen-year-old restoration that cost a total of about $2,000.00. He has also modified it so that it runs on either propane or gasoline. When he runs on propane he does it for about one-half of what you and I pay to run our vehicles. Most of us would buy a new vehicle, put down 25% or 30% with down payment or trade, then with finance costs wind up paying seven or eight times what Paul pays for good, attractive transportation.

I would like to briefly summarize Paul and Ann's lifestyle change, then show you in simple mathematical form what they are accomplishing with **MMM**.

Three years ago Paul was a forty-year-old, $60,000.00-a-year corporate executive, living in a prestigious suburban area. The general cost of living and job pressures were eating away at his financial well-being and physical health.

Today Paul and Ann have an eighty-acre farm that is totally paid for, and luxurious living is within their grasp. Their farm produces 90% of all their food requirements, plus, within a year or so, they expect to produce enough extra meat and poultry to give them a $10,000.00-a-year income from their farm enterprise. They have three sources of electricity—wind power, gas-driven generator, and rural electric; also, three sources of heat—propane gas, wood-burning stoves, and free-standing passive solar furnace. (Cost of this last item was about $800.00, plus a little ingenuity and labor.)

In all, I would say this family has security. Power blackouts or outages, energy and food shortages, economic down-turns or crisis would have very little effect, if any, on this modern pioneering family. Also, Paul has taken a pressure-free job with a firm that treats him very well, and is within easy commuting distance of his farm. In theory, he is now making considerably less money than he did as an executive. But surprise! Paul is actually earning more spendable money now than he did before.

Let's take a look at it in simple mathematics:

Former Executive Job:

$5,000.00 per month salary ($60,000.00 per year)	$5,000.00
Taxes (poor shelters)	$1,500.00
Housing (mortgage payment, taxes, maintenance, other utilities)	$1,300.00
Food (family of four)	$ 600.00
Automobiles (payments, upkeep, insurance, gasoline)	$ 800.00
Entertainment (clubs, associations, family, restaurants, others)	$ 600.00
Balance left:	**$ 200.00**

New Lifestyle (Employment and Farm):

$2,333.00 per month salary ($28,000.00 per year)	$2,333.00
Taxes (good shelters)	$ 400.00
Housing (maintenance, taxes, other utilities low because of their other sources)	$ 250.00
Food (family of four—cost of raising only)	$ 80.00
Automobiles (upkeep, insurance, gasoline)	$ 160.00
Entertainment (farm will provide many; school, church, small community, all less costly)	$ 100.00
Feed for Animals (they also have good grazing land)	$ 300.00
Balance left:	**$1,043.00**

As you can readily see, Paul and Ann cut their income in half, but realize *over five times the spendable balance left!* Besides that, their farm will be worth an astronomical amount in the near future, with building costs and land values continuously soaring.

I don't advocate that you run out and sell your house tomorrow, and immediately try to duplicate Paul and Ann's efforts, because what was a general shared interest for them and their family may not be the same for you and your family. But if you can just relate to a few of the ingenious things they did, you will be on your way to effectively using **MMM** to become an *Armchair Millionaire.*

12. SUGGESTED READING

The following pages list just a few of the hundreds of excellent books and magazines that could be considered required reading for the new business entrepreneur or *Armchair Millionaire.* Also listed are some of the names and addresses of distributorships available, also some mail order opportunities if that is your inclination.

BOOKS

Winning Through Intimidation
by Robert J. Ringer
Fawcett Crest Book
Subject: General

How to Wake Up the Financial Genius Inside You
by Mark Oliver Haroldson
Mark O. Haroldson, Inc.
Salt Lake City, UT 84117
Subject: Real Estate Investment

Better Shopper
Box 91, Box FW
Ithaca, NY 14850
($2.50 postpaid—checks should be

made out to Cornell University)
Subject: Grocery Purchasing

How to Prepare for the Coming Crash
by Robert L. Preston
Hawkes Publications
Salt Lake City, UT 84107
Subject: Depression and How to Profit

The Possible Dream
by Charles Paul Conn
Berkley Medallion Book
Subject: Amway (Some information would fit other distributorships)

Special Note: All of the Dr. Norman Vincent Peale books have been an inspiration to me.

I have listed only four financial magazines here, but there are many others that have excellent articles and opportunities within. You should be able to find any of these at a book and magazine store.

Income Opportunities
229 Park Avenue South
New York, NY 10003

Spare Time
Kipen Publishing Corporation
5810 West Oklahoma Avenue
Milwaukee, WI 53219

Money-Making Opportunities
11071 Ventura Boulevard
Studio City, CA 91604

Specialty Salesman
304 North Michigan Avenue
Chicago, IL 60601

The following companies are among the leaders in the distributorship business; also, they will encourage you to build your own dealer network.

Amway Corporation
Ada, MI 49355

Shaklee Corporation
P.O. Box 10066
Palo Alto, CA 94303

AMS/OIL, Inc.
AMS/OIL Building
Superior, WI 54880

Beeline Fashion
100 Beeline Drive
Bensonville, IL 60106

Figurettes, Inc.
P.O. Box 1029
Scottsdale, AZ 85252

These are two mail order guidance books; however, I must caution you that mail order without a serious businesslike approach can be dangerous. But if you observe the proper perspective, it can be most stimulating and profitable.

The Lazy Man's Way to Riches
by Joe Karbo
17105 South Pacific
Sunset Beach, CA 90742

Dollars in Your Mailbox
by Ernest P. Weckesser, Ph.D.
10576 Temple Road
Dunkirk, NY 14048

I hope *Armchair Millionaire* will supply you with a method of starting your own home-operated business for a more successful, happy, and self-gratifying future. And perhaps the topics I have discussed will trigger your imagination and creativity to develop a much-needed service that will fulfill all the dreams and ambitions you possess. For with perseverance and **MMM**, financial success is within your reach starting right now.

May your future get brighter and brighter with each passing day. . . .